TRANSFORM YOUR LIFE

YOUR LIFE

Expert Advice,
Practical Tools, and
Personal Stories

A Co-Creative Book, Contributed to By:

Scott Allen
Madeline Altabe, Ph.D.
Berenice Andrews
Andrew Appel
Tracey Ashcraft, M.A.
Rachael J. Avery
Laura Barrette Shannon
Zan Benham
Janice Carlin, M.M.
Karen Castle, A.P., D.O.M.
Kayla Cole
Linda Commito
Jim Del Vecchio, M.S.
Alexander Dolin
Sylvia Edmonds
Elizabeth Egan, M.Ed.
Rebecca Edwards
Dana Feldmeier
Chara Free, R.Ph.
Arielle Giordano, M.Ed.
Jeff Gitterman

Dolores Gozzi
Steve Harding
Terez Hartmann
Carol Hasbrook
Victoria Hawkins, LCSW
Dana Houk, M.S.
Frannie Hoffman
Elliott Eli Jackson
Colleen Jais
Elena Jones
Alison J. Kay, Ph.D.
Dianne Kipp
Toni LaMotta
Ivanska Laureano-Tate
Jami Lin
Gary Loper
Kandy Magnotti
Marty Finkelstein, D.C.
Juliet Mathison
Joran Slane Oppelt

Howard Peiper, N.D.
Darcey Pollard
Janet Reynolds
Emily Rivera
Joeel A. Rivera, M.Ed.
Natalie Rivera
Spencer Rouse
Gregg Sanderson
Kelly Slevin, M.T.P.
Noelle Sterne, Ph.D.
Linda Stewart
Tammy Taylor
Elasa Tina Tiernan Sherbs
Camille Titone
Jim Toole
Luz Treviño, M.Ed.
Angelica Love Valentine
Deserie Valloreo
Kathy Wallace
Maggie Webber

ISBN 978-1-60166-042-8

TRANSFORMATION
PUBLISHING

Published and distributed by
Transformation Publishing
www.transformation-publishing.com

CONTENTS

INTRODUCTION

Standing in my front yard, I stare for a long time trying to discern the color of my grass. I consider the cliché about "the other side." Time passes as I take in more of the view. Then I notice a crack across my vision. From my glasses, I pull away pieces of broken lenses — green in color — revealing the brown, weary, thirsty grass that has invaded my lawn. I wonder who had put it there. What horrible gardener had duped me into paying for such a mess? I look down at my calloused hands, covered in soil, holding remnants of green lenses.

How could this be happening? How is this *my* lawn? How are these *my* hands? I turn to the driveway, and I look at my reflection in the side of my car; I don't recognize the woman staring at me. For a moment, I consider rushing to find superglue and frantically repairing my lenses. But then I come to the realization that I'm trying to deny what I truly desire by reciting an old cliché—"the grass is always greener on the other side"—and convincing myself that I shouldn't chase greener pastures. In truth, I wasn't using it to help me remain grateful for what I have; I was falling back on it in fear of losing what I know.

With this profound realization, I look at my reflection once more and the woman has shifted. I am no longer looking down, slumped with the weight of the world on my shoulders. A new woman is looking at me eagerly, with the fire of transformation in her eyes.

I was unsure of what the "other side" would hold for me, but I was certain that I had to leave my side — before I allowed the temptation of the status quo and self-denial to color my world once again.

And so began a rapid unraveling of my life: With the end of the string in my hand, I was running like fire. After dismantling literally every part of the life I had created, my cloak had been unwoven and I stood revealed and refreshed (and, well, naked), in awe of my own freedom and in integrity with my true Self.

Transformation happens. Sometimes we seek it, and other times it is thrust upon us.

Sometimes it sneaks up on you after years of quiet suffering and denial, as it did for me. Other times it is the inevitable side effect of a life struck by a sudden tsunami of unwanted change, grief, and/or pain. In either case, once transformation begins it *usually* unfolds rapidly. But, in this process, there are those who cling desperately to "what was," like a terrified butterfly unwilling to let go of the empty casing that once housed the caterpillar. Life is exhausting, painful, and dark when trapped in the cell created by our resistance to change.

To resist change is to resist the universal force that drives all of life.

We are experiencing a time of unprecedented transformation. More and more individuals are experiencing life-changing shifts, but it's more than that—it's happening on a global scale. It's as if all of humanity is awakening. Some believe the rapid change we're observing is due to economic conditions or technological advancement, while others believe the cause is a greater energetic shift taking place on Earth.

In any case, if you are experiencing or seeking transformation, *you are not alone.*

Life can be full of challenges and obstacles that can feel overwhelming and impossible to surmount. Even once we embrace transformation, the process isn't always pretty. Imagine what it's like for a caterpillar to release everything in order to become the butterfly. (See the chapter "Metamorphosis: The True Story" for elaboration.) However, there is always something to be grateful for, and every day is an opportunity for a spark of inspiration to trigger the call for transformation deep in our heart and soul. In fact, many scientific studies have proven that a simple change in perspective can impact every aspect of our lives, from our relationships and careers to our overall happiness.

We cannot always control what happens in our lives, but we *can* control how we respond to every situation and development. We can see our challenges as curses, or we can allow them to inspire blessings in our lives. And, that's exactly what the real-life heroes and experts in this book did—they battled through the trenches of despair and difficulty and emerged victorious to tell us the tale.

About the Book

What do a college student studying psychology and a shamanic healer in her 80s have in common? They are both coauthors in this truly collaborative book, which is a diverse mosaic of authors from around the world—offering 60 unique perspectives on love and hope, strength and perseverance, and living and thriving. Each chapter tells the true-life tale of overcoming real-world challenges, from addiction to abuse, illness to loss. Your heart will open as authors share their personal stories of rebirth and reveal how they allowed their pain to inspire their purpose.

You'll have the tools to live your *best* life when you discover the powerful, proven methods and techniques compiled by experts who teach from the heart and build upon their own life experiences. After reading this book, you'll feel empowered to embrace transformation, turn tragedy into triumph and achievement, and express more of your true, authentic Self.

Read straight through or meander to the chapters you feel drawn to explore in the moment, and glean their unique insights and inspiration. You can even open to a random page and search for a hidden message just for you.

Bearing the depths of one's soul and telling the true story of personal transformation creates a ripple effect of inspiration.*

Allow the authors of *Transform Your Life!* to pay it forward by sharing their hearts, souls, stories, and wisdom with you. You may even discover the key that unlocks the power of your own story contained within the pages of this transformational book.

Thank you for transforming with us!

— Natalie Rivera, Publisher

---

*The ripple continues... YOU can pay it forward by sharing the inspiration contained within this book with your family and friends. We want to touch the hearts of as many people as possible and encourage them to embrace their transformation. Below are ideas for ways you can help spread the word:

- Buy a copy for someone in your life who could use a dose of inspiration
- Recommend *Transform Your Life!* to people you know
- Join us on Facebook (www.facebook.com/transformyourlifebook) and SHARE it with your friends
- Leave us a review at: Amazon.com, BN.com, GoodReads.com
- Email us your questions or feedback (publisher@transformation-publishing.com)
- Share YOUR story with others (or submit it to us for a chance to have it published in a future book!)
- Download the eBook through Kindle, Nook, iTunes, Android, and leave feedback

THANK YOU for transforming with us!
Your support allows us to continue to follow our purpose.

SECTION I:
OVERCOMING AND THRIVING

Finding Purpose in Death

By Joeel A. Rivera

We all have loved ones, who come into our lives to help us grow, and sometimes when they leave us the lessons become even more powerful. Many people find it hard to look through the pain of loss to reveal the blessings that often lie within the curse. Don't get me wrong, I still miss my brother and all the experiences that I would have wanted to share with him, even if I see the greater purpose that he has inspired in my life through his death. As an expression of gratitude, I share this letter to my beloved brother, Daniel.

Daniel,

I write this with tears, but these tears are different than the ones that I carried for many years. I can now say that I truly understand your last words before your death. It seems like yesterday we were sitting across from each other in your room, practicing how to read each other's minds. People thought we were twins because of our resemblance and the way that we communicated and understood each other without words. It seemed that from an early age you understood life, as if you were an old soul, knowledgeable and compassionate about making the world a better place.

We always found ways to encourage each other through the challenging times.

Even when I had given up on my belief in myself after failing my first year in college, you encouraged me and reminded me of my potential.

That night of July 1ˢᵗ 1999, when you were 17 and I 19, we sat on the roots of several-hundred-year-old Ceiba trees at two o'clock in the morning, probably as many people had before us. We were in a deep discussion about life. You looked at me as if you were talking to my soul. You explained that you had a deep feeling that you would die young and you knew that you would make a larger impact through your death than through life. I questioned you, but you could not explain the feeling. We sat there in silence as we both started to weep, as if mourning the inevitable.

Two days later I was awoken by the sentence that still takes my breath away to think about. "Wake up, Daniel has been in a car accident." I desperately asked if you were okay, just to find silence. However, I continued to probe and received the answer that in my heart I already knew. Why you? I asked, wishing that it was me instead. My emotions and my body sat still in time, not knowing what to think or feel. I remember coming back home from your funeral as it started to rain. As if by instinct, I started to run in the rain, just like we had so many times as children. It almost felt as if through the rain you were washing away my tears.

Those words lingered in my mind, "I will have a bigger impact through death." You never explained the pain. I was lost, desperate, overcome with the grief of losing my brother, my best friend, my guide. I developed severe high blood pressure, was sleeping two hours a day, developed ulcers, and lost over 25 pounds.

Several months later I reached my breaking point after getting in a car accident that nearly took my life. I remember being on my knees at home screaming, talking to you, desperate for answers. That night I saw you in my dream — you looked at me with the same look that you gave me that night under the tree. Through tears of your own you explained that you were okay and that you were paving the way for me and that you no longer wanted me to suffer. I woke up with a sense of peace and purpose. This sense drove me to go back to school and finish my Bachelor's with a 3.8, my Master's with a 3.9, and a 4.0 as I complete the dissertation for my Ph.D. It drove me to open a counseling center for youth to honor your name, as I had promised the day after that dream. Through your death I have mentored, motivated, and shifted thousands of youth, individuals, and families, and will continue to share the light that you blessed me with.

Ten years after your passing, in a state of sleep, I had a dream that was so vivid that it seemed real. I saw myself living many different lives and in each one of them I would die a traumatic death. At the end of the last one it was as if my spirit was lifted and I experienced your presence, your light. I explained that I didn't see how I could live these experiences again because each time I come back more confused — it had created a fog in my being. You stated that in the next life you would come back with me and die an early death to shift me and change my path so that I would not have to go through the cycle again. I asked why you would do that, and you answered that I had done the same for you. And, that it is exactly what you did. At the point of my life when you passed away, I was reckless and confused, and through your death, you shifted me from dying an early, or traumatic, death. It is as if you had a contract with my soul.

As my brother, my best friend, and soul mate I thank you for all the wonderful moments that you gave me in my development. I thank you because the tears that I shed now are of joy and gratitude for your sacrifice. I finally understand your words, "I will make a larger impact through death." I know that the greatest thing that I can do for you is make the impact in the world that you so desired. As I promised so many years ago, through my life your name and spirit will continue live and be shared, Daniel Rivera.

Love you eternally!

Joeel A. Rivera

The pain and hurt in life are not there to hold you back, they are there to inspire your greatness. By embracing the lessons and finding meaning and hope within them, you inspire others to do the same.

Joeel A Rivera, M.Ed., is a visionary, entrepreneur, and motivational speaker. After failing his freshman year of college, losing his brother, and being in a nearly fatal car accident, Joeel was inspired to return to college, where he earned a Master's Degree in Education and is currently completing his dissertation for his Ph.D. in Psychology, with an emphasis on happiness. Joeel opened a nonprofit teen center in honor of his brother and developed curriculums for the Juvenile Justice System. In almost a decade, Joeel has reached over ten thousand people as an educator, entrepreneur, speaker, and consultant. He is Vice President of Transformation Services, Inc. and author of *Enlightened Relationships: Secrets to True Love and Happiness.* Visit www.joeelandnatalie.com.

When Your Life Changes Forever

By Elliott Eli Jackson

My life has changed forever. Yes, a transformation, and you can have one, too. You can, from this point forth, "Create a New Reality." It is the very reason you are reading this book. Something inside of you is searching—and it is your spirit. At this very moment, your essence is seeking ways and means to improve your inner and outer being. The good news is it will find a way. For you are a creator, and it is time for you to remember this truth. One or more aspects of your fourfold being—spiritual, physical, emotional, mental—or a combination of these aspects is reaching out for guidance and assistance, and it is being provided. Therefore, your life is moving in a positive direction right NOW!

I am going to share with you a glimpse into what I was like before I began to change. Then I will name four spiritual universal tools that have been given to us all to assist in our transformation process.

Lost

Along with my wife Diane, I travel the globe presenting the "Create Your Reality" workshop and promoting the bestselling books, *From God to You: Absolute Truth* and *The Sapiential Discourses Universal Wisdom* book series. There have been many obstacles along the way. Sometimes people think that I always have been on a spiritual path. This is true in some respects. All of us, including *you*, are on a continuing spiritual journey. However, before my life became as it stands now, I was lost, I was broken into many pieces and unhappy. My personal vibration was very low, and with this low vibration came addiction to hardcore drugs and alcohol. To me the world was dirty—a dirty place with dirty people, doing dirty deeds.

I understand now that I created this vision. I told lies, stole from those I loved, spent every dime on drugs, and was wasting away on the inside. I knocked on death's door. Even though I knew many people who were happy in their lives, I did not believe that their happiness was genuine.

Then I made the decision to get involved with a 12 Step program, and I began to change little by little. But I did not understand that I was going through a spiritual process, and I did not act accordingly. I started working as a counselor for drug addicts, alcoholics, troubled teens, torn families, and couples on the verge of divorce. I helped assist many with anger issues, yet I was angry myself. Later, I worked with the criminally insane at a maximum security prison, but I was still making poor choices in regard to relationships. And there was wreckage in other areas of my life. I did not see much hope. I became depressed and, strangely, I did not see any connection between my lack of happiness and my spiritual condition. I thought that the universe/God had it out for me. I was in dire straits.

Then the universe sent a person to help me seek spiritual enlightenment/truth. That woman is my wife Diane. I suggest the same opportunity is there for you—to meet someone (or "some ones") who will point you toward uplifting ways. The universe places positive, high vibrational people into all of our lives. They just pop up and present us with information that can change our lives. They guide us through forks or junctures in the road of life that can take us home. If we take these paths using the information given to us, we will no longer be lost. We are all given many universal opportunities to shift and change what we are doing and how we are doing it. These also are the times when our biggest hurdles appear. It could be the loss of a job or a loved one, the ending/changing of a relationship. These occurrences lead to a new direction.

I am referring to the points in life when things are no longer working. You feel as if something is not quite right. These points may even happen when there is some measure of success. But on a spiritual level you feel that there is more to it all than what meets the eye. It becomes apparent that changes must be made in the way that you are living and interacting with others.

The Universal Tools

Through Diane's guidance, I began to venture into New Age classes and seminars. During the course of investigating these wonderful ways of thinking and looking at life and healing, the universe pointed me to use four universal tools that changed my life: **meditation, healing family ties, audible prayer, and taking care of self—all aspects**. If you use them, you can change your life, too.

Meditation gave me the ability to better deal with those things that I believed were problems and issues. It has allowed me to understand on a deeper level that I am not disconnected from others. Additionally, during meditation, the spinal cord and muscles are being worked on at a higher level, and the ratio of neutrons to protons within the body is being adjusted.

Healing family ties has made it possible for me to have deep, meaningful relationships with others and resolve my karmic issues. I began by contacting my direct bloodline, both living and deceased. For the ones who had transitioned, I wrote letters to say the things I needed to say and could not or did not express while they were alive.

Audible prayer helps me to express gratitude for that which I have, have had, and will have. Through prayer, it becomes easier to speak to the Source of all things about anything, and I am able to release the thought that I am being judged for my words. This process results in a new freedom and a new relationship with the universe.

Taking care of self—all aspects means recognizing that we live forever through a combination of physical and spiritual lifetimes or existences. This was channeled to me as the Sublime Law of Forever in my book *The Sapiential Discourses Universal Wisdom*. Once a deeper understanding of who and what I am reached down into my conscious and subconscious being, better eating habits, the need for some kind of exercise, and use of vitamins and supplements became more apparent to me. Remember, if you don't take care of yourself, nobody else will.

The knowledge to change is within your reach if you are willing to use the tools and follow higher guidance. Embrace the journey.

Elliott Eli Jackson is the internationally known channel of Source energy, and the bestselling author of *From God to You: Absolute Truth* and *The Sapiential Discourses Universal Wisdom* book series. He is an inspirational speaker, Reiki Master/Teacher, Ordained Minister, and contributes monthly to the The Sedona Journal of Emergence magazine. Elliott and his wife Diane travel the globe doing book signings, the Create Your Reality workshop, and Private Sessions with Source, through Elliott, which thousands have attended. Private Sessions with Source, are also available via phone/video chat. Visit www.quantummatrixcenter.com, FB & Twitter. Elliott and his wife live in the Chicago area.

The Truth Set Me Free

By Chara Free

Once I was told, "The truth shall set you free," and in that moment, something within me stirred. Nothing had stirred inside of me for a very, very long time. Then the dam broke. I cried for two days, and I let out what was killing me inside.

When I married my first husband, my niece told me I looked like Cinderella. I felt like Cinderella, marrying the handsome prince. We were a beautiful couple, and it looked like we had it all. We were both pharmacists, and we had a home in Boca Raton, FL, with a pool, a boat and many friends. We also had unresolved childhood issues. Once we got married, we started partying and letting our true colors shine. We started fighting and neither of us had any coping skills that were healthy. We partied and poly-substance abuse was an everyday occurrence. We also both took prescription pain killers. I took them for my headaches, and he took them for his back. The last five years of our marriage I thought I had discovered a cure-all for my "unresolved issues."

This, of course, led to a multitude of problems. I was hooked, and I could not stop. I liked how they made me feel. I liked that they numbed out the world. My tolerance kept building, and I took more pills. This got sloppy and my actions had consequences, like getting a divorce, getting fired, and putting myself in a situation that landed me in ICU.

This kind of thing was already taboo, but it was more complicated in my case, as I was a pharmacist with a drug problem. My week vacation in ICU allowed me to finally see that my way was not working for me. Faced with almost losing my life, I decided right then and there to make a change. And change I did.

Moving Forward

I changed everything about how I thought, felt, and behaved. I did this by going to rehab (again), going to 12 Step meetings (I still go), and learning a new way to live my life so I could be happy and healthy in my own skin without needing a drink or a drug. Days turned into months, months into years. I was given a second chance and I was determined to make it great. I remarried and had two beautiful baby boys. I became a stay-at-home mom. My husband, also sober when I met him, was a doctor. Life was moving in the direction of my dreams.

Then, one day, everything changed. I found those pain killers in my husband's briefcase. I freaked out. I confronted him. It was awful for quite some time, unpredictable and insane. Things continued to get worse, and then I understood that I had an obligation to report him. No matter how scared I was to do it, I did an intervention on him, and he went away for help. That was three years ago. He never came home. A tsunami hit me out of nowhere, fast and hard.

His actions caused damage that he ignored. I dealt with it solely. I chose to tell his staff what happened and that he was not coming back to the medical practice that we built . They lost their jobs. Some of them did not get work again for a long time. The patients lost their doctor. The ripple effect had just begun. I filed bankruptcy. Then, I moved across the state to be in a larger job pool and closer to family.

I began working full time at a hospital, with crazy hours, a new babysitter, and aftercare at the boys' schools. The boys already lost their father, and now I was working all the time. I had to work extra to pay back the trustees just to keep my furniture. It was a radical change for us, and it was stressful.

We moved to a house after the first year, and life started to settle. I divorced my second husband. He claimed that he could not face life, although the tests he insisted on proved there was nothing physically wrong with him. And I began the repair process and started picking up the pieces the tsunami left behind.

Coping Skills

From the minute I found the pills in the briefcase, until now, I have used fundamental coping skills to survive. <u>Every single day</u>, my sons were my inspiration to put one foot in front of the other. I have done whatever has been necessary to make sure each of their precious needs have been met.

And I took care of myself. I exercised and got massages, stretched at night, and went to the chiropractor. I saw a therapist, stayed connected to my recovery program, reached out to my friends and family, and asked for help (and took it). These were my basic tools, and during difficult times, I have learned that I must do all of these and then some. I would go to the beach and sit for a few minutes or take a walk. I took hot baths and let "Calgon take me away." I meditated more and learned to go within to find peace. I've read more books and listened to guidance from my favorite mentors. I began to journal and write. I had fun with friends along the way.

I never stopped dreaming about my future and doing what I could to feel good about it. I have made it through the tsunami. I have grieved and grown. I have accepted what has happened, and I am standing in the most empowered place I have ever been. My first husband recently committed suicide and my second husband is hiding away from the world. I learned that I simply had to make a decision about what I wanted and, in doing the footwork, I made it through the fire.

The tools work for me every time.

Life if precious and life is short. I am living each day as best I can "in the present." I cannot wait to see what happens next. I can fine-tune the details in my life and teach my children and others there is <u>always</u> a solution . The purpose of life is joy and my purpose now is to spread joy and love where I am able. I am grateful for everything that I have been through to make me who I am today. I am grateful for learning I have the power, anytime, anywhere, to make a decision about my circumstances. Once I make a decision, mountains move.

Chara Free, R.Ph., is a mother of two boys, studied at The Florida State University, and graduated with BS Pharm from Nova Southeastern University. She currently practices as a Clinical Pharmacist, with sixteen years of experience. Chara resides in Ormond Beach, FL. Contact freec23@aol.com.

What's Your Story?
The Importance of Perspective

By Laura Barrette Shannon

Most people think that their life story is just a succession of events that can't be changed. This is partially true. The past is a combination of what has happened and, more importantly, your subjective interpretation of those events. How you narrate your personal history will directly affect how you feel about yourself and influence how others see you.

What is your story? Your story is what you tell yourself and others about your life. We do this all the time when we meet new people. The longer we know them, the more we fill the story with whole chapters and characters we have met. The key is to know that while you can't change the past, you can change how you interpret it. You are the narrator of your life, so you have the power to change the viewpoint of the story.

Changing the viewpoint of your story involves looking at past events in a different way. We live in a world of duality. Any event can be seen as positive or negative, depending on what is emphasized. Think about your life story. Do you feel like you've been a victim of circumstance, or have you learned to triumph through adversity? Depending on how you interpret the past, it can be viewed as tragic or epic.

For example, I could tell my story as a tragedy, featuring me as the star victim: The best years of my life were taken from me when I became disabled in my late 20s due to a problem in my brainstem. I was in pain all the time and was stuck in a cycle of depression. My condition eventually required brain surgery. One month before the surgery, my only daughter was tragically killed in an auto accident. My life has been one bad nightmare. Nothing ever goes my way. How can I ever be happy? I hate my life!

This is a "Woe is me!" type story of victimization.

Or, I can tell it as an epic story starring me as the hero: Many years ago, I went through some emotional and physical trauma. These events provided an atmosphere of deep introspection of life and acted as a catalyst for self-transformation. When I became physically disabled it gave me time to practice meditation, and learn to connect with my authentic self. The loss of my daughter taught me to respect the precious gift of life. I came to realize that I was disrespecting this gift by complaining and being pessimistic. I learned that I can be happy no matter what happened in the past, regardless of current life circumstances, or whatever the future unfolds. I am grateful for the challenges of my past, because it has given me the opportunity to grow into who I am today.

This is a "Life is good!" type story of triumph
through adversity.

It is important to understand that both versions of the story are just different perspectives of the same past events. The past hasn't changed; the way I think about it has changed. What I choose to verbally emphasize has changed. How I revised my storyline altered my character in the story, shifting it from a victim to a hero. This shifted who I am, transforming my life.

Become aware of how you talk about yourself. Your every word defines who you want the world to see and reinforces your self-image. How you reflect upon and share your story will affect your self-esteem and how others see you. Don't play the victim in your life story, you won't feel like a victim, and you won't be perceived as a victim.

If you keep the narration focused on unlimited potential for the future, lessons from past adversity, appreciation for the people who come and go, and gratitude for life itself, you will not only enjoy life more, you will be a joy to be around.

How to Change Your Story

Today ask yourself, "What's my story?" If you don't like the story, then change it. Don't fabricate lies, just reframe how you describe past events and who you are. If you had past adversity or tragedy, begin to speak only of the lessons you have learned. Don't focus on the pain. Focus on how you used the experience to grow as a person or how you learned more about yourself and life in the process.

Take time to sit down and rewrite your life story. It may take many rewrites before you eliminate all of the negative narration that you have been accustomed to telling yourself and others. At least start with one happier, more positive version of your story. You will be able to rewrite it as often and as much as you desire. There are numerous ways to tell any story. Make yours a happy one, even if you don't believe it yet.

Story lines can be changed as easily as transforming your words.

Transform "I can't do that." into "I'll give it a try!"

Transform "I'm not good at ____." into "I'll do my best."

Transform "I'm not very good at ____." into "I do it because I enjoy it."

Transform "I am a victim of circumstances." into "My experiences have taught me valuable lessons."

Transform "Life is difficult." into "Life provides many learning opportunities."

Begin to use story lines that cast you as the hero.

"I learned so much going through _____. I am truly grateful for the experience."

"Going through the loss of _____ really taught me how I should never take things for granted."

"I learned that I can grow stronger through adversity."

"I am not afraid to follow my dreams, because I know that failure is just a step on the path and another notch in my belt of experience."

"I know I can be happy no matter what happens in my life."

"Life is good!"

You are the writer and the director; choose what to zoom in on or cut out. You can describe your character any way you wish. It's your life! You write your own story, make it a happy one and watch your life transform.

Laura Barrette Shannon is a poet, philosopher, and dreamer. Her work includes the poetry collection, *Awakening Perception* (2006), which chronicles her journey from hell to happiness, and *Be Happy Now: Simple Steps for Enjoying Life* (2012), which explains practical techniques for creating a happier life. Laura is a happy free spirit, despite the loss of her daughter, chronic health issues, and bipolar disorder. When she is not writing, you may find her discussing poetry in the park, counting butterflies in the backyard, or singing karaoke. Laura lives a life of joy and love with her husband and two dogs in Largo, FL. Visit behappynowbook.blogspot.com.

Lifting the Fog

By Kelly Slevin

When the time came to write this chapter, I had to review my life stories to determine which ones were the most monumental in transforming my whole "Self." Then I had to decide which of those stories I was brave enough to share. The process of choosing also has been transformational because I had the recurring revelation that this whole life we live is one big process of transformations, ever-changing, ever-evolving.

The saying, "You learn something new every day," is not entirely accurate; we are learning new things every second. The most important part of the process is to remember to be aware of the lessons.

My biggest lessons came from experiences throughout my whole life. I was a sickly child, born with a double ureter, and I had surgery at age 4 after months of recurring infections and courses of antibiotics. My immune system took a beating, and I've been extra-susceptible to infections and other illness since that time. I've also been in a battle with migraines for 20 years.

When I was 22, I took a trip to the ER by ambulance. I thought I was having a heart attack, but it turned out to be a panic attack. A trip to my doctor diagnosed me with Generalized Anxiety Disorder. He started me on a very common, strong benzodiazepine. I had gone to nursing school, so I knew that people built up a tolerance to this drug, and I made a conscious effort to take as little as possible. For years, it was my security blanket. When my heart began to race, I could count on that little pill to calm me down. When I couldn't sleep because my mind was racing, I could count on that little pill. When I was feeling completely overwhelmed, I could count on that little pill. I became dependent.

I took my tiny doses four to six times a day. I continued to struggle with migraines and headaches. I did my best to function as normal as possible given the way I felt, and I was diagnosed with Fibromyalgia along the way. I also did my best to cope with my own internal struggle. Taking this drug went against everything I believed in, but I was scared to stop taking it for fear that I would have a real heart attack. I assumed that I would have to take this drug for the rest of my life or, if I wanted to stop taking it, I would have to check into a hospital to detox.

I decided to cut back on the benzodiazepine a few years ago in an attempt to wean myself off. I was able to decrease my daily dosage by two-thirds but not able to stop completely. I just could not seem to rid myself of this drug's grip on me. It was driving me crazy, so I finally made the solid decision at the end of 2013 to wean myself off it altogether. I asked my sister to keep an eye on me. I made a schedule and planned out how I would decrease using what I had. I thought it would take a month or so, but I broke myself completely free of the drug in three days. I was so angry that I had let this go on for so long that I just wanted to stop, and I was ready to put myself through whatever it took to let go.

The first two days of decrease were rough. The anxiety was atrocious, the tightness in my chest was scary. On the third day, I could start to feel major changes in my cognition, my overall perception, my strength, my appetite, my vision, and my whole body. I didn't sleep for five days. I started to have true emotions again; they had been covered up with what I call "benzo fog." I knew that I was going to have to learn how to feel all over again—and to cope with those feelings. However, it was like I was completely reborn, renewed, refreshed, and rejuvenated. Most importantly, there was a huge sense of pride in this accomplishment. My fog had lifted! And I was able to see how beautiful life was once again. I had a newfound gratitude for all that I had been through, where I was going, and who I am. My head also hurt less often. I was ecstatic!

I had dealt with other people's drug addictions in my personal and professional life, but I had no idea that I was addicted to this benzodiazepine for nearly 15 years. It made me sad that I had blank spots in my memory from that time period, and it made me sad that I had walked around for so long in that fog. I felt like I had to apologize to everyone who had ever been a part of my life. I wasn't myself. I vowed never to touch that drug again. I also vowed to let others know my story and experience. And I vowed to remind others that our mind is powerful beyond our comprehension. We can accomplish absolutely anything we set out to do.

Each day is a bright new day as I feel healthier and more energetic than I have since high school. I let go of the guilt and shame I was carrying for those 15 years. I now work hard to keep my anxieties in check with breathing techniques, yoga, meditation, a healthier diet, and exercise.

I had to relearn what I already knew before getting caught up in the pharmaceutical world that most Western physicians adhere to these days: I truly believe that we were put on this Earth with absolutely everything we need to survive and triumph in this lifetime. Only when we accept and live mindfully with that inherent truth will we properly thrive as individuals and altogether as a global unit.

Kelly Slevin, MTP, BA, PBT is the founder of the Sunflower Institute and has a Master's in Transpersonal Psychology. She is a passionate writer, teacher, adventure-seeker and works hard to push herself and others to overcome obstacles we all face. You can read about Kelly and find all of her works at www.kellyslevin.com.

In the Blink of an Eye, Life Changes

By Janet Reynolds

Sometimes your life can change in the blink of an eye and, if you didn't see what was coming, it can rattle your cage for quite a while afterward. "Drastic" is the word I often use to describe what happened when I was 32 and divorced with two sons.

At the time, I had a personal and business relationship with one of my clients and was very much in love with him. We merged our two businesses into one office space and our relationship grew; we were intimate and considering a long-term partnership. I had been on birth control for 12 years, and I would have tests every six months to detect any problems. One morning the phone rang, and it was Dr. G. on the line to tell me I had cancer of the uterus. It was in stage four, and I needed to come to his office. My head started spinning, and all I could hear was the word "cancer." I thought I was going to pass out.

I pulled myself together and told him I would be there the next day. I got off the phone and sat down. I was home by myself because my boys had already left for school. I picked the phone up and called Charlie, whom I had been seeing for three years. I told him what the doctor had said and asked him to go with me the next morning. We met with Dr. G. and he explained everything he possibly could about the "cancer." He also informed me that I needed to have a hysterectomy — and I had to do it soon. How could this be happening? I was speechless.

You see, in my heart I knew I was going to have a daughter. I even knew what her name was going to be. A hysterectomy would alter everything I knew to be true about my life and would eliminate the possibility of giving birth to another child. I remember telling the doctor that I would get back to him with my answer because I needed to go home and think.

The Decision

I did more than think. I talked with Charlie that evening and told him I wanted one more baby. I then asked him what his feelings were on this, knowing I was asking for quite a lot, because Charlie was married with four children of his own. I understood what I was doing and, while that did not make it right, he had always indicated that he would leave his wife to marry me. After much conversation, he did agree to support me getting pregnant. I knew above all that I wanted that daughter — the girl who would be called Maiteland after my mother.

I had another meeting with Dr. G. to let him know what I wanted to do. I told him I hoped to deliver one more child before the hysterectomy. He was not happy with my decision and gave me many warnings. At the same time, he also told me what kind of surgery might help safely deliver a baby, given my cancerous uterus.

I never did tell my sons that I had cancer but I did inform them I needed to have a procedure. Their dad wasn't in the picture for them, and I didn't want them to think they were going to lose their mother, too.

After the surgery I had one more checkup with Dr. G., who let me know that everything looked good, but that there were no guarantees. He informed me that, were I to get pregnant, I needed to retain a lawyer for a living will and find a new doctor. Dr. G. had decided to give up his medical practice, so he recommended Dr. B., a surgeon who could handle any complications of my pregnancy.

The lawyer I would have to find myself. When a doctor tells you to write your will, a rather large lump lodges in your stomach. But I was adamant about continuing with my plan to have another child. I met with Dr. B. who outlined the tests I would need to have over the course of my pregnancy, just to make sure everything was going smoothly. The doctor also was able to recommend an attorney friend of his to handle the living will.

Dr. B. put me on another birth control method for a year because he thought that my body needed to recover at least that long from the procedure. Then I had two miscarriages. It had been 11 years since my last son's birth and, even though I was healthy, my body was not accepting the pregnancy.

The Joy and Gratitude

It was January, and Charlie and I were in New York. I just knew

I was pregnant. I remember so vividly being in that hotel room, telling him I was pregnant and asking if he was still onboard with it. I knew he had agreed well over a year ago, but I wanted his feelings on the situation now. I was prepared to do whatever I had to do if he didn't agree now. He let me know it was fine. You know there are times when things are meant to be, even when situations are hard.

I gave birth to my daughter in September of that year. I was happy she was born in September because it was the same month as my own birthday. Exactly as I knew I would—from the time I was eight years old—I named my beautiful daughter "Maiteland Marie."

Three months later, I finally had the hysterectomy.

Even in the face of a cancer diagnosis, I wouldn't have changed a thing. Today, I feel I am cured, and I am so very thankful for how everything transpired. I still make sure to have the tests on schedule, but decades have now passed and my daughter has made me a grandmother twice over.

When something is meant to be, the Universe somehow lines everything up in our favor. In my case, I had exactly the doctors I needed, who were willing to go along with my wishes. And I am so grateful to my daughter's father for allowing me to take that chance with his own future. What could have been a death sentence for me ended up bringing new life into this world. And here I am all these years later, adding this milestone to my ongoing life story, which isn't over yet—not by a long shot.

Rev. Janet M. Reynolds is a Certified Spirit Medium and ordained minister with a private practice in Tampa, FL. She specializes in practical channeled guidance from the spirit world, through private intuitive consultations and group séance gatherings. She holds a mediumship certification through the College of Metaphysical Studies and has studied at the Arthur Finlay College in England. She is Certified in Clinical Hypnotherapy and has obtained advanced instruction in hypnosis and past life regression at the Edgar Cayce Foundation in Virginia. She has studied medical intuition with Caroline Myss and Dr. Shealy and is a certified Reiki Master. Contact Janet at janet@bluefeather.net.

Honoring Colby:
Rebuilding My Life THROUGH Loss

By Kandy Magotti

I'll never forget the day my brother died. Like a time machine, it's as if my memory transports me right back to that moment in the hospital room with my mother, father, husband, me, and my lifeless brother. With the energy of the bright sunrays shining through the hospital room window, there I stood in my darkest hour reeling from utter emotional pain and disbelief feeling like it was a dream and a nightmare all in one unfortunate reality.

"My brother is dead and he is never coming back" I spoke internally. On July 9, 2005, Colby Jonathan Cox, my brother and one and only sibling, died at the age of 26 from a rare disease called Adrenoleukodystrophy (ALD for short) changing my life and world forever. I watched my brother, who I loved in many ways like my own child as a consequence of the many years spent caring for him, die a slow, degenerative, and painful death. With a shattered spirit and grief stricken heart I was now forced to face the rest of my life adjusting to a new existence as an "only child." How on earth was I to do that?

ALD—three little letters that have had such an enormous impact on my life. ALD is a slow, progressive, degenerative killer that ultimately renders its victims in a vegetative state to the point where they can no longer move, speak, or see. ALD is a neurological brain disorder that destroys myelin, the protective sheath that surrounds the brain's neurons, the nerve cells that allow us to think and to control our muscles. ALD is an X-linked genetic disorder that is passed down from mother to son. If the cards that life has dealt decide to place ALD in your DNA, the chances of being a female carrier are 50/50 and the chances of being a male victim are 50/50. The odds were against us so it seems. My mother is a carrier, her mother was a carrier, and I too am a carrier. Two of my mother's four brothers died from ALD as did my mother's only son: my brother...

The days leading up to his death are etched on my soul. Many weeks, days, and hours were spent at the hospital. My mother basically lived there in that sterile room. I'll never forget the smell. I would come almost daily to give her a break and spend one-on-one time with him. He couldn't move. He couldn't eat. He couldn't speak. But he could hear. I recorded myself on a cassette tape expressing all the things I wanted to say to him, most importantly how much I loved him. I reminisced about stories from our childhood and the special memories only siblings could "get". I sang "our song," one that only he and I shared. I told him he deserved to have eternal peace after a lifetime of struggle. "It's ok to let go my sweet brother," I whispered, "it's ok…"

I knew he could hear it all because every time the recording came to an end, his face would twitch and his breathing became more labored. I would quickly rewind the tape, place the headphones on his ears, and press play. He would immediately return to stillness. We must have replayed that tape a thousand times up until that night…

My brother and I have a very special connection. You see, we were born on the exact same day six years apart. So when he left this earth, I felt it *before* the call even came through the next morning. I woke up in the middle of the night crying because I *felt* my brother had died. I convinced myself it was only a nightmare and fell back asleep. Early the next morning, a little after 6 a.m., my mother called from that hospital room to tell me Colby had died in his sleep sometime during the middle of the night. What I obviously had already known in my heart was now confirmed in my mind.

Because of his existence, because of all we went through as a family, because I needed to find a way to honor his life, I searched my heart and soul for my purpose. What was that experience all for I asked my Source? There *has* to be a reason…Three years after his death in a rare moment of quiet after my twin daughters were born, I dared to ask myself that question out loud. I heard a voice as clear and calm as the bright blue sky after the perfect storm reply, *"grief counselor."* I looked around the room to see who was speaking to me. I was home alone with my children sound asleep. While I may have been alone in that room physically, I know I was not alone spiritually…

My brother died nearly 10 years ago and, although there is still sadness in my heart, I can honestly say the pain of the experience is gone. I am emotionally COMPLETE with the loss. How did I do it you may ask? Well, in many different ways AND in the most important way... by making the <u>choice</u> to walk THROUGH my pain rather than finding ways to avoid it. I did and continue to do the spiritual and therapeutic <u>work</u> required to process my life THROUGH my loss experiences. It's a choice I make every day...

There is an enormous difference in how you experience the rest of your life after any loss with sadness versus with pain.

Where my memories of Colby once caused me pain, they now hold a space of peace, solace, and gratitude. My strong desire to honor my brother's earthly experience and existence navigated me towards a career, *my calling*, that now allows me the ability to share what I've learned in order to successfully help my clients facilitate their loss experiences and pain. There are no quick fixes and it is work, however, walking THROUGH it *begins* with a choice. I chose to gain a truer, more authentic Life THROUGH Loss™ — and you can too.

In your stillness, ask yourself out loud, "Do I want to cope with loss or do I want a Life THROUGH Loss™? Don't be surprised if your question is answered...

Kandy Magnotti is the founder of Life THROUGH Loss, LLC and is a Pre-Licensed Marriage & Family Therapist, a Certified Grief Recovery Specialist®, and a Grief, Loss, and Trauma Facilitator. She holds a Bachelor's Degree from Rutgers University and earned her Master's in Marriage and Family Therapy at Argosy University. After having a wonderful 10 year career in the medical and pharmaceutical industries, her last of which was with the pharmaceutical giant Pfizer, she was financially successful but spiritually unfulfilled. A personal tragedy has led her to the work of grief therapy and recovery in addition to becoming spiritually fulfilled. Visit www.lifethroughloss.com.

I AM Somebody: My Childhood Promise

By Luz Treviño

I'm sure you've had rough times and asked yourself, "When is this going to end? Is there a light at the end of this never-ending tunnel?" Well, I'm here to tell you that I've not only had moments like this, but a whole decade of my life felt this way. During that period, I had a near-death accident and one of my coworkers actually gave me a mug that read, "I'm Having One of Those Decades." It made me realize that I wasn't paying attention to my life. I was on autopilot, and during those 10 years I did not allow myself to reflect on my current life experiences or my childhood. Then I remembered *a promise I made to myself at very young age:* **"One day I am going to be somebody,"** and this is where the story of my awakening and true gratitude for life actually begins.

I was born in Muskegon, MI, but I don't recall the time I spent there because my sister, brother, and I moved to New York City when I was just a toddler. I attended school up to second grade and, at eight years old, I was looking forward to third grade when we were told to say goodbye to our friends in church; we were moving to Puerto Rico the following day. I cried myself to sleep that night, and on the airplane I pressed my forehead against the window watching the lights of New York disappear as I said to myself, "I'm coming back."

In Puerto Rico, after moving from one place to another, my oldest sister and I were placed in a Catholic boarding school. When the nuns gave us a tour, I was scared to see that the dormitory consisted of two long rows of twin beds very close to each other. Lying in bed my first night, I placed my right hand under the pillow and pressed the right side of my face hard on that pillow. I didn't want that hand to come out. You see, I sucked two of my fingers, and I was afraid the other girls would notice and make fun of me. I cried myself to sleep once again. I missed my dad, my little sister, who was born while we were in New York City, and my brother.

I was 10, and I was repeating third grade. I didn't know Spanish either, but I caught up quickly. The nuns made sure of that! We didn't get many visits from family. Owning a car was a luxury and they lived far from the school. Once every few months a lady would pick us up so that we could spend time with our youngest sister, who insisted on seeing us. I made the best of my situation. At the age of 13, I graduated from this school with high honors, and my Dad took us to another boarding school, closer to where he lived.

I was so excited (and nervous at the same time) to see the school, make new friends, have more visits from Dad...and then all of a sudden I froze...I looked up and noticed these large letters all across the building, "Colegio de Niñas Huerfanas." (School for Orphan Girls). I realized then that the "boarding school" where I spent the past four years actually was an orphanage. So many images and thoughts crossed my mind. "I was not an orphan. Why? Why?" Then it all made sense: There were rich girls from town who attended the school but didn't live there. That's why they made fun of us...That's why we had to clean the classrooms and hallways, deal with some abusive nuns, jump out of bed at 5:00 to get ready and help a younger girl, wash the uniforms in huge concrete basins, read to the nuns while they ate; and the list goes on. I felt so little, like **NOTHING**.

My sister and I looked at our Dad and asked him, "WHY?" He told us he was working hard to save money to get a place for us. We told him we wanted to leave with him. We pleaded and cried, but to no avail. It was not possible, he told us. That night, as I had done every night, I got on my knees and prayed and cried. **"I'm going to be somebody,"** I repeated to myself over and over again until I fell asleep. We were in that next orphanage for one year, and then we moved with our Dad and my brother into a two-bedroom tiny "doll house," as we called it. I was so happy. I went to a regular public school and loved it. I even realized that I was thankful to the nuns, for they instilled in my heart a love for learning and school.

When I graduated from high school, I kept the promise I had made to myself on the airplane when I was eight. I went back to New York City with a goal in mind: **"I'm going to be somebody,"** and I knew education was the path to get there. That was my goal, and I vowed that if I ever had children, I would do my best to give them what I didn't have. *They would be somebody.*

I began my studies, not without difficult moments, but my determination and God's promise to me kept me moving forward. Whenever I felt defeated or ready to give up, I would go back to the image of a 10-year-old child kneeling before the cross, weeping. This was a constant reminder throughout my life that no matter what I went through, I was never alone. God was always with me, giving me strength.

My experiences as a child did not make me a bitter, resentful, or an angry woman. On the contrary, they prepared me to become the strong woman I am today and to be able to face all the events that unfolded during the decade that inspired my soon-to-be-published book, *I've Had One of Those Decades.* To be able to face each challenge life has brought my way with strength and determination; for this, I am grateful.

We are all "Somebody."

Luz E. Treviño was born in Muskegon, Michigan. At the age of three, her family moved to NYC and then to Puerto Rico. She graduated from high school in Puerto Rico and moved back to NYC and enrolled in college. Luz has a Master's in Education and a Master's in School/District Administration. She worked for 32 years for the NYC Department of Education. Luz taught in a South Bronx high school and retired as a high school administrator. Luz raised five girls, is retired, and lives in Boca Raton, FL and currently works part time at Florida Atlantic University, College of Education. Contact decadesofmylife@gmail.com.

Life After Abuse:
Finding Hope through Forgiveness

By Kayla Cole

I believe that the direction of a person's life can be determined by one small decision. For me, the catalyst was an itch. At the time, I was 5 years old and watching cartoons. I just scratched the itch without thinking anything of it. But unbeknownst to me at the time, I was being watched by my stepfather, and that itch sparked a sexual interest in his mind, one that prompted his decision to start abusing me. For the next few years I was taught to perform sexual acts that no child my age should ever experience. I was molested and mentally abused, yet I didn't realize anything was wrong with the situation until I was older. I was never threatened or forced into anything. It was "our secret" for 11 years before anybody in my life found out the truth.

I wrote my Mom a letter during my sophomore year of high school and left it in her truck. I knew I was going to crush my family's world, but I couldn't continue hurting myself because of his actions. I made a decision to stop accepting my reality as having to live with abuse. I wanted it to change. However, everyone thought *he* would change now that the problem was "in the open." He became very good at walking the walk and talking the talk, but he continued. The physical touches stopped, but the stalking, videotaping, and mental abuse continued. At 15, I was afraid that if I kept bringing it up I'd be taken away from my Mom and family, so I found ways to cope. I was stuck in the mindset that I had "no way out." My world was small and unchanging, even though I tried to find ways to escape it.

The toll his abuse took on me did not show up physically like bruises. I was the one who left the marks on my body. I needed something to calm my mind from racing thoughts and discovered one night that when I cut my skin I focused on that specific pain rather than the intrusive thoughts. The self-injury then led to an eating disorder. In six months I lost 60 pounds. My nights were flooded with hate toward myself, and the cutting continued, too. I had anxiety anytime I was supposed to eat, which led to more cutting and more depression. I was spiraling downhill fast, and nobody around me caught it.

And the abuse continued: He spied on me in the bathroom by using a small hidden video recorder. He chipped away part of my bedroom door frame so he could get down on all fours naked and pleasure himself while I was in my bedroom. If I went out back of our farm, he would find an excuse to mow the grass where I was. One night I even remember him being in my bedroom while I was sleeping, and I prayed that when I rolled over he would go away. I worked at the same retail store as he did, but during the night shift, and often I had to come home and spend all day alone with him in the house. I literally had no escape from him.

When I reached my sophomore year in college, I woke up consciously and realized I needed a way out of the life I was living. He pushed my Mom and me too far, so we moved out of the house. By this time, I no longer had an eating disorder or cut myself; I had decided that my body was not going to be controlled by any man or hurt by my own unstable thinking again.

This was a big step forward, but I still had another critical problem to contend with: I saw things—people and figures—that were not really there. I wasn't technically hallucinating because I was 100 percent certain that they weren't real. They were like a child's imaginary friends, but these fictional characters weren't nice to me. I had been seeing them for years, and they were extremely distracting, upsetting my normal life. Finally, I told a good friend of mine about this problem, and he gave me some advice. He said, "Ask them why they are there. Ask what their purpose is."

The next time it happened I did just that, and the response had a profound impact on my healing journey. These imagined people and their associated story lines would preempt me from remembering the abuse. They kept my mind occupied. Since the age of 7, my brain had found a way to protect my conscious mind from my reality of abuse! After the questioning, the visions began to happen less and less, and it was time to come to terms with what had happened in my childhood and move on.

I was 20 years old at the time, and I knew that I had to find forgiveness in my heart. I forgave my family for how I felt betrayed. I also forgive my stepfather. It's not easy to forgive the man who took away your childhood innocence, but it was the best decision I ever made. The letter I wrote to him talked about how I was accepting my past and said that I forgave him for everything. I even thanked him at one point, saying he opened my life to a world of helping other people find peace from similar abuse. I finally found the positive in all of the negative experiences I had endured. I walked up to my stepfather at work one night, after avoiding him for weeks, and handed him my letter. As I walked away I felt like I was able to leave behind my anxiety and depression and everything negative about my life with him in it. It was exhilarating, and I encourage anyone who's been abused to do the same.

I don't blame my family or myself for what happened to me. My abuse happened at the hands of one man. It was his decision to touch me and mentally abuse me. The only decision I made was to remain closed off in my world.

Abuse doesn't have to define you.

It is nothing to be ashamed of, and it is definitely not a good reason to hurt yourself. At some point, you must determine that — regardless of the circumstances surrounding the abuse — there is hope. There is something positive that will come from the experience when you make the decision to transform your life.

Kayla Cole is a freelance writer and a psychology graduate from the University of South Florida. She believes her purpose in life is to guide others to achieve their own goals, dreams, and aspirations. She writes a weekly flyer for her company called L.I.F.E. (Live It Fully Everyday) to motivate her coworkers. Being a fitness enthusiast she also co-writes about her journey to a healthier lifestyle on WordPress at swolesisters.wordpress.com. Her latest project is an abuse recovery workbook which she hopes will inspire other to grow from their past and transform their lives for a positive future.

The Slipstream of Life:
Finding Inspiration through Grief and Loss

By Colleen Jais

Life is change. It started the moment we were born, and it has consumed every moment since. Whether we are aware of it or not. We recognize change when there is too much of it in our lives and it causes pain or suffering. Consequently, if there isn't enough change in our lives, we often become bored and consciously or unconsciously prompt something to create movement again.

If we do nothing, and there are no changes in our life, we die. Whether it is an emotional death or a physical death—life without change is impossible. However, life with change can be difficult. So painful in fact, that it can break our spirit and our belief in ourselves and the ability we have to manage life. To live our life well and full is to become aware of change, accept it, and welcome it. We need to understand change and then use it to transition into the next stage of the journey.

To be able to transition from painful change to a state where we are able to fulfill our hopes and dreams is within our reach, and that capability is part of who we are right now.

However, some of us need a little jumpstart to understand what makes us tick or how, as individuals, we process information and ultimately change. One way is through images and words.

Looking at images to stimulate the imagination and facilitate a new way of thinking can help us to learn how to process and then pull up and out of ourselves—our own guidebook for living the very best life possible. Viewing images can start a chain reaction of more images in our mind, and may also then kindle new feelings and emotions, stimulating the imagination. These new connections may open a door or set forth a path that we can use to guide us to channel changes from within. Moreover, as different connections are being made, maybe an image will spark a memory, or maybe it will elicit hope or rekindle a long-forgotten dream.

The words we associate with images are meant to encourage us to fill in the blanks with our own bridges of understanding and messaging. Words also may be used to raise the question, "What does that really mean?" which then leads us off in a new direction that we may not have thought about before. Once the mind becomes engaged, then the soul can begin to integrate fresh impressions, and can begin to recognize change in a new way.

> *Looking at images and reading poetry, or any thought provoking words or phrases, can open your soul – the "you" of you – so you may begin to grow and expand into new ways of connecting and living.*

If faced with enough stimuli, we can change the way we think or feel about a situation. With these new connections, we may be able to crack apart the walls of pain and release the chains that hold us from moving forward in life. Fresh insights can give us the necessary links to transition from the painful part of change into the slipstream of change, in other words, the flow of your life. The slipstream identifies the point or place in life in which everything is "as it should be." Things fall into place in the slipstream – a promotion, winning a race, a traffic-free commute, an unexpected phone call, or anything that makes you feel good, feel as if you are in the highest flow of positive energy possible.

> *The slipstream is like a band of energy, a highway of insight and possibility, exposing the path to the purpose and direction of your life.*

For some, their purpose stays hidden, the elusive slipstream calls but can't be accessed. There may be many questions:

- "What is my purpose?" or "Where is my purpose?"
- "How do I find that place in my life where all things feel right, the place where I can feel most at home, at my very best?"
- How do I find my slipstream, my real life, the one that is buried like a treasure?"
- "Is there a map?" and "How do I read it?"

Your life can flow in the slipstream if you understand that the process of change is nothing more than a navigation system that is designed to "right" your course and put you into alignment with your life purpose. Not the purpose of "all of life," but rather, *your* life.

Outside stimuli, such as images and words, create the bridges of understanding for the mind to formulate the connections needed to heal old wounds and help decrease anticipated uncertainty. Transition then becomes a conscious event, something that can be experienced in the present moment, not feared because of some past event, or dreaded because of an unknown future outcome. Transition is about being in the NOW and coping with events that shape the present. We can then acknowledge change as the map for navigating into the slipstream and shifting the course of our lives for the better.

Sometimes the impression of one color can open a doorway; sometimes it takes a whole palette.

Colleen Jais, is author of *Into the Slipstream: A Guide to Finding Inspiration through Grief, Loss and Change*. For Colleen, life is a study of transition; life itself becoming her resume. An artist living in the real world, Colleen has always worn many hats to fulfill the practical nature of the journey of daily life and all of its evolutions. A writer, an artist, a wife, a mother, a daughter, a sister, business owner, and entrepreneur, whose passage through these transitions is the fabric of her being, Colleen shows that each "change" along the way is an extension of her ability to assimilate and then access the wisdom born of life experience. This "war chest of experience" has guided Colleen through life from small town girl to a well-traveled capable soul. Contact cmjais@yahoo.com.

Good Grief!

By Frannie Hoffman

Death is not extinguishing the light; it is only putting out the lamp because the dawn has come. — Rabindranath Tagore

The early and sudden death of my husband, Steve, has forever changed me. My journey through unimaginable depths of grief has brought me, finally, to a place of greater awareness, understanding, and appreciation for the precious gifts life continues to offer me.

I believe that there are not enough preparations or instructions in the world that are adequate to help us understand the true depths of grief. Facing the challenges that come when we lose a loved one sometimes feels unbearable but we must do it. We begin again courageously as we take baby steps to create a new life while honoring the past.

As a spiritual counselor, I have helped many work through grief and other emotions that leave us feeling stuck, out of balance, and disconnected from our true selves. Yet none of my personal or professional experiences prepared me for what lay ahead — physically, emotionally or spiritually — in the wake of Steve's transition.

My years of meditation and mindful living helped me to feel deeply, everything that Steve's transition brought to me. I wanted to run away to Bali like Elizabeth Gilbert describes in her book *Eat, Pray, Love*. I was left with it all, and I let it bring me to my knees.

There was a stronger force within me that would reach into my body and mind. It would open me up. I would walk on, sometimes blind and deaf and with so much pain and fear. I allowed my God to take the lead of this new dance, and then I felt Spirit carry me into a mind that had only silence. I embraced this unknown place within me. Here I would get nourished and listen to the birds' song of new life. I would rest in a quiet mind and let this inner something — God,

Universe, Presence — help me go on and tell my story.

My beloved left his body from an aneurism and yet I know now that it was his way to go – quick and clean. I am sure he didn't want to leave me, but his soul was finished and his mission with me complete. He had voiced to me a few times during his last day that this was the best day of his life. It was the worst day of my life.

Grief was knocking on my door. It consumed me like a hungry animal, wild and merciless. I had no choice but to let it in and take over every cell of my being. I had no idea that I would crumble into millions of pieces. I felt I had no choice but to let go and allow grief to teach me everything I did not know.

Love Remembers

It was so hard to open my eyes to the daylight. I felt as if I was underneath something so heavy that I was struggling for breath. I could not see anything but darkness and the pain to think a thought shoved me deeply into the abyss. There was no sound but my own. I cried and cried the longing for him. I was crushed under the wall of grief. It had fallen on top of me. All of me was crushed and, even though it was him who died, I was dead and left upon the floor like a shattered piece of porcelain. I was scattered upon the ground in a million pieces. Where did I go? Where was I now? I was lost in the valley of sorrow.

Then one day I woke up from the dream. I was taken by the hand of spirit, and every piece of me joined back into the perfect form of the One. I was whole again. I was wrapped in the arms of the Divine, never forgotten; only loved.

He was there, more alive than ever before. I saw him with every part of me. I felt him inside and all around me. I knew that everything was okay and the plan was unfolding without my effort. All I had to do was trust in God. This perfect creator who knows all things had not forgotten me. This love was all that is real. This dream of separation became the doorway to everything. The plan was unfolding without my effort. All I had to do was trust in God.

I remembered to allow myself to breathe. The silence of the mind began to fill my heart with what is real. Here I was kissed most sweetly by the Divine. I took the hand of what was waiting for me. This sacred journey we are on, where death was only a doorway into new life. Love could never die. His body was gone, yet more of him was here to dance this life with me. I felt him in this world. He spoke to me through nature, music, sunsets, clouds, and through the voice and touch of my fellow human beings and all creation. He showed me who I truly was.

His exit from his body brought me home to the One. Now as I give myself to spirit and allow God's ever present being to guide my life, I am free. I am free to share this love with all of humanity. No one is separate from me as I walk on. I now can choose to see the light of love in all of my brothers and sisters. I bow to this experience for now I can see who I truly am. Thank you, thank you for this life where love does not exclude anyone or anything. This world we are a part of is a reflection of the One. The one perfect being that is pure love takes my hand even when I fall. For I have a choice to join with spirit, where all of my loved ones have returned as life shows me the way. Here I am not forgotten for love remembers.

(Excerpt from Frannie Hoffman's upcoming book *Good Grief! Loss – The Doorway to New Life*.)

 Frannie Hoffman is a spiritual intuitive, educator and a transformational leader. Over the last twenty years, she has touched the lives of thousands across U.S. and Canada through her Circle of Light meditations, spiritual counseling practice, writings and compelling seminars and workshops. June 10th, 2013 brought the sudden death of Frannie's husband and soul-mate, Steve. The ensuing year presented her with the most challenging and profoundly transformational times of her life. To share her experiences and insights she is currently working on her next book, *Good Grief! Loss–The Doorway to New Life*. Frannie is also the author of *From Modeling Clothes to Modeling Self*. Visit www.FrannieHoffman.com.

SECTION II:
THE POWER OF THOUGHT

Beyond Success

By *Jeff Gitterman with Andrew Appel*

Most classic success stories go something like this:

"I had nothing, but then discovered a new way of thinking, turned my life around, and got everything I ever wanted..."

I could tell you one such story. I went from debt and depression to everything I'd ever wanted – in the space of about two years. It all started back in 1997, when I was just another New Jersey insurance salesman, trying to support a wife and two small children on $26,000 a year, falling months behind with the mortgage payments, scared and unsure of my future. I was hiding my car at the end of every day because a finance company told me they were coming to repossess it. Debt collectors were constantly calling, and my wife at the time was close to a nervous breakdown. I had credit card debt, mortgage debt, car loans. Things looked pretty bleak. And then one day...I changed my way of thinking...and within only two years...but wait a minute. That's actually not what this is about.

One day, I was getting out of my car and about to walk into a prospect's house to try and sell a term life policy. I was way behind on my bills, and my mind was going on and on about how much I needed the sale. Desperation poured out of me as I caught my reflection in the car window. I stopped, looked hard at that reflection and said to myself, "Who would want to buy anything from you? Look at how desperate you look!"

And then I figured something out. I had an epiphany – or an enlightened moment, whatever you want to call it, where I realized I was going about things completely the wrong way. I realized that I was focused on what I wanted, but not on what I was willing to give in order to get what I wanted, and as long as I approached my business in this way, I would never succeed.

I thought of the successful people in my office and realized that to some extent, they all had a confidence about themselves that I sorely lacked. And so I decided in that moment that I needed to drop my desperate, needy attitude and walk into this prospect's house with the confidence of someone who didn't want anything. I took one last look at my reflection and saw that I had taken on an air of serenity, and that's when I began to realize that I really didn't need anything, that deep down there was nothing for me to get. I dropped my need to make a sale. I became still and quiet.

I soon began to approach more of my clients this way, putting all my attention on them, without any desire or expectation for myself personally. And to my amazement, my meetings really started to transform and my success as a financial advisor grew exponentially.

From my observations and experience as a financial advisor, it seems that many people are in the same rut that I was in. They know what they want to get, but no one along the way ever told them that they'd have to be willing to give something first. Many, if not most of us have been taught to focus on getting the big dollars and the big job, whatever it is, but we rarely come to understand that what we get really has nothing to do with what we want to get.

If you're solely focused on what you want to get, chances are you'll get nothing. But when you figure out what you want to give and what you want to be — you can then have whatever you want. It's a weird paradox, but the truth is that when you let go of wanting anything, you can have everything.

Although it sounds like a bit of a cliché, I was able to see firsthand as I was going through my own crisis around wealth and success that the more I gave to others; the more I received in return. I quickly began accomplishing more in the world and my income grew substantially. In addition to starting my own financial firm, I also became the chairman of the advisory board to The Autism Center of New Jersey Medical School, and started a fundraiser that we now hold every year, which to date has raised over a million dollars for autism research.

Unfortunately, too many of us spend our whole lives waiting to get something from the world so that we can show up as the person we always knew we could be. Deep in our hearts we think there's something missing. But when we flip that mindset, we can discover that by becoming a giver rather than a taker, we can become agents for change in the world. In the end, it was only through giving to others that I was able to find the kind of happiness that I was really looking for. This is one of the main things I learned when I began to look for what might lie "beyond success."

Jeff Gitterman (top) and Andrew Appel (bottom) are the co-founders of Beyond Success, a coaching and consulting company that brings more holistic ideas to the world of business and finance. Jeff is also an award winning financial advisor and the founder and CEO of Gitterman & Associates Wealth Management. He has been featured in numerous TV, print and radio programs, including Money Magazine, CNN, Financial Advisor Magazine, Transformation Magazine, New Jersey Business Journal, London Glossy and Affluent Magazine, among others. In 2004, he was honored by Fortune Small Business Magazine as "One of Our Nation's Best Bosses."

Prior to co-founding Beyond Success, Andrew spent nearly a decade in the entertainment industry, both as an actor and in production and development for a variety of film and television companies in California and New York. He is a Phi Beta Kappa graduate of the University of Wisconsin-Madison, and has also spent time at Oxford University and USC Graduate Film School. For more information, please visit: www.BeyondSuccessConsulting.com and www. gawmllc.com. Jeff and Andrew are also Associate Producers of the feature documentary film Planetary: www.PlanetaryCollective.com.

Listening to the Voice Within

By Karen Castle

Are you open to receiving inner guidance when the time comes to take action and change your life? Does this process excite you or does it result in trepidation because you are taking a risk?

Our trajectory and sense of fulfillment in life depends on how well we can hear and respond to that inner voice, so it's important to take steps to build trust in the process, which ultimately will align us with a path toward wholeness. There always will be challenges to face and obstacles to overcome, but the upside is that these tests provide the clues necessary to steer us in the right direction. Trusting our inner compass and letting go of fears can facilitate the most powerful life transformations imaginable. A simple analogy is a ship at sea that has a predetermined destination but changes its course in response to weather conditions, such as storms, as they arise. Similarly, we can reach our destination and full potential in life by allowing inner guidance to help us grow and become stronger by adapting to circumstances along the way.

On this journey, I have found two basic tools that have the power to lessen fear of transformation and help us tap into the inner wisdom that, in turn, will motivate us to achieve our soul's purpose. They are myth and metaphor, and together they help us to process and make sense of the information from everyday life.

The Power of Myth and Metaphor

Metaphor is beneficial because it uses symbols to help us relate. When we identify with symbols that have outer meaning, we are more likely to raise our awareness and gain insight that can open our mind and change our thoughts. Myth is equally powerful for our overall growth and development because it assists with the realization that life is not about reaching a destination; rather, it is about the journey. *Myth teaches us to learn and grow from challenges.* Both Joseph Campbell, the well-known mythologist, and Carl Jung, the famous

Swiss psychologist, used myth and symbolism to help explain and conceptualize human thought processes.

Indeed, my journey would not be as expansive without knowledge of myth and metaphor. Ten years ago, in a deep meditation called Holotropic Breathwork, I connected with an ancient feminine archetype named Inanna. This symbolic dream left me with a longing to know more. Through listening to my inner guidance, I discovered the ancient myth of a goddess from the Sumerian culture and have since written two books that serve as an everyday reminder to recognize and remember the paradoxical aspects of life.

All myth, no matter what the cultural background, is fundamental. It dominates our human experience and provides us with good examples of our deepest instinctual experience. Myth is an articulated structure of symbolism that assists humanity in overcoming adversity. Since the beginning of ancient times, myth and folklore have outlived many actual cultures because their timeless tales teach us about survival and withstanding human suffering.

Overcoming Adversity in Life

Life is an ongoing transformative experience. Ideally we want to be happy, and to experience triumph and joy. We want to sail through life avoiding obstacles and stormy weather, yet the reality is we all experience challenges. Yet overcoming adversity can deepen our sense of fulfillment, especially when we have myth and metaphor to reference along the way. I know this firsthand from my own rollercoaster ride through life.

We all have life stories to share. For example, I had multiple auto accidents that occurred in my twenties and resulted in a permanent disability. Granted, I had plenty of days wallowing in self-pity, but I made a choice not to view this as a hindrance. Instead, I was motivated to seek natural options and find an "alternative" treatment solution. I changed my career from accounting to Chinese medicine and acupuncture, and now 14 years later I continue to be rewarded by assisting other people to heal and feel better.

I experienced another personal tragedy when my stepson died of suicide. Losing this special young man was devastating, especially because I have a son. I struggled to stay strong and support my husband—we were only married a few months—but I found myself deeply depressed. With the simple slogan "This too shall pass," I was able to trust an inner knowing that this was my dark night of the soul and to embrace the process of transformation. Again, this was easier said than done. My only recourse was my determination and willingness to continue forward and trust inner guidance.

Today, my personal story continues beyond physical and mental injuries. I've struggled financially along with many others in the recent chaotic economy, but my inner knowing has helped me withstand rough seas to reach calmer water. I identified with shedding layers of unnecessary attachments and focused on a practice of courage and fortitude, which has resulted in a deeper understanding of my whole Self. As I write these words, I am working at sea on board a ship to help educate and treat people from all over the world with acupuncture. Every day I am riddled with tests and trials, but I have grown exponentially by leaving my comfort zone, relying on my inner guidance, and looking to my favorite myths and metaphors for support along the way, such as Inanna.

Myths and metaphors are like mirrors for our soul to look upon to deepen, expand, and embrace life with all that happens. We can use them to let go of preconceived belief systems and connect with inner guidance to influence the overall outcome and trajectory of our life course.

When we sharpen our awareness and tap into inner wisdom, it serves as a guide that clears the path for our growth and transformation. When we cannot see what is ahead it can be scary, but with a deep trust and inner knowing — that voice telling us to embrace the mysteries of life — we will find fulfillment within.

Life is like a ship at sea, and the opportunity to be guided is a choice we make. The lighthouse is there awaiting and welcoming our return, and to achieve wholeness and inner peace we must follow the light home by listening to the voice within.

Karen Castle is an Acupuncturist, a Transformational Coach and a Holotropic Breathwork Practitioner. Her Master's degree in both Transpersonal Psychology and Oriental Medicine is the basis behind her expertise in the mind, body, spirit approach to health and wholeness. Karen hosts monthly workshops offering a style of Breathwork that opens one to his/her inner wisdom. She is author of *Unveiling the Modern Goddess* and *The Sacred Union*. Currently, Karen is a PhD candidate at Wisdom Graduate School and is working on the high seas integrating her knowledge to help others heal and awaken to self-knowledge. For more info, visit www.karencastle.com.

Change Your Thoughts, Transform Your Life

By Deserie Valloreo

Life is a journey of endless possibilities. Thinking about who you want to be, what you want to do, and where you want to go on your journey can be so exciting!

Of course, not everyone thinks this way. In fact, many people do not see life this way at all. They drudge through each day as if it were a chore rather than the true gift that it is.

Then there are the people who have experienced the treachery and hopelessness of living life in a cycle of negativity and found a way to break out of it. I am one of these people.

I had been trained since childhood to think the worst and to live in fear. Just a couple years ago, while talking on the phone with my mother, she expressed concern because I had started writing and performing music around town. "You aren't going to stop doing your natural health business are you? YOU CAN'T do that." Then it hit me. I had been told the words "you can't" my entire life.

It was an epiphany. A big smile spread across my face, and I replied to my mother, "No mom, I won't shut down my business." She was relieved.

I believe this is my parents' way of trying to protect me: "If we teach her to be cautious, afraid and distrustful of people, she won't get hurt."

The problem with this model is that when our thoughts are always focused on what can go wrong, we diminish the chances for things to go right.

This has been a HUGE struggle for me in personal relationships. Being so afraid the other person will hurt me made me unable to receive love and unable to truly give love. Fortunately, I became aware of these negative ways of thinking, which enabled me to take conscious action to work to "unlearn" the bad stuff and retrain my mind to be open to possibilities rather than closed with fear.

Strategies for Success

One way to do this is by using a technique I learned during my yoga training, and that is to become the observer in your own mind. Create space between your emotions and your reactions. If something makes you angry, sit and observe yourself feeling the anger. It is okay to feel anger. It is how you react to the anger that makes the difference between being happy and being upset. If you observe the anger as a witness, you can experience it and let it go rather than react and create even more negative energy for yourself and others.

Sometimes I am too open and I do feel "hurt," but that is just my ego sulking. My true Self, the one observing the sulking, knows that this experience is just a part of the journey. My ego chooses to define my experiences as good or bad, when really it is just an experience—and that is all it is.

In order for us to know joy and love, we must know the sadness of feeling hurt. What is the point in experiencing anything if it is just one continuous act of sameness?

A favorite quote of mine comes from the book "The Untethered Soul." It reads:

> *"The only thing there is to get from life is the growth that comes from experiencing it. Life itself is your career, and your interaction with life is your most meaningful relationship."*

When you change the way you think, it affects your outlook and attitude. The expression "think positive" is basically saying if you think positive, meaning you truly BELIEVE in a positive outcome, it is more likely to happen.

An extremely important factor in changing the way you experience life is being very clear on your intentions. To do this, you must be present in each moment. If you are not paying attention to the moment, it is lost forever. You won't even have a memory of it because you weren't paying attention when that moment happened in the first place.

You can use a variety of tools to help you stay focused on the current moment and reinforce your intentions.

One way to become clear on your intentions and focus on the present moment is to ask yourself, for each task that you perform throughout the day, "What is the purpose of this task?" "Why am I doing it?" This can be challenging to do at first, but like most things, consistent practice will make it easier.

You also can use this in other areas of your life. For example, I was struggling on how to approach a situation with someone I felt had done me wrong. This individual was trying to insert himself back into my life. When I recognized that my intention was to be his friend, I was able to state this to the person and ask his intention. It helped to clarify and communicate what I expected from the situation and gave the other person the opportunity to do the same.

In addition, affirmations or mantras can help you focus on your intentions. These are phrases or statements repeated on a frequent basis. Affirmations can have amazing effects in overcoming personal blocks, limitations, or harmful habits.

I went through a period a few years ago where I was feeling defeated and tired all the time. A friend suggested I try creating a mantra or affirmation to help turn things around. He said it changed his life, so I decided to give it a try.

The idea is to identify what you are lacking or desiring in your life and turn it into a positive statement. I used "I am happy. I am healthy. I am prosperous." (I also added "I am grateful") as my mantra. I repeated it to myself every morning before I got out of bed. This mantra helped me realize how much our thoughts and perceptions dictate our lives. It was a powerful, positive turning point in my life.

Imagine you are observing your feelings rather than reacting to them, you are focused on each moment of your life and you are clear on your purpose and intentions. How do you think this will affect your life?

You will have replaced the negative noise in your head with positive statements. You will have changed your thinking and changed your life.

Deserie Valloreo is a Natural Health Advocate and Certified Clinical Herbalist. She is featured in over 200 eHow.com instructional videos on natural remedies. Her company, HerbalWise, LLC, is a global resource for natural health education and remedies for health and home. People suffering from pain, fatigue, insomnia and other health concerns, find natural solutions by attending Deserie's workshops and using her natural remedies. In addition, Deserie is the founder of Holistic Workshop Academy whose mission is empowering holistic practitioners to turn their passion to help others into profit for their business. She is also the leader of the Holistic Network of Tampa Bay. Visit www.HerbalWise.net or Deserie@HerbalWise.net.

Using Gratitude as a Gateway to Abundance

By Jim Del Vecchio

My devotion to gratitude started in the intensive care unit of a hospital after a major operation. There were complications after the surgery. My doctor told me 20 years later 90 percent of the people who have the level of kidney function that I had are dead within one year. Every day seemed to bring some new challenge, and the doctors were stumped. One day a nurse came into the room to start her shift. She complained about her life. She complained about the traffic, the grocery store, her employer, her coworkers, and so on. It seemed many people, including me, did not appreciate what they have. I resolved if I ever got healthy again, I would concentrate on being grateful for what I have, even in the face of less-than-perfect conditions. I even experimented with being grateful when something does not go my way.

After getting out of the hospital, I went back to college and got a Master's in Counseling so I could specialize in career or vocational counseling. While working, I developed an expertise in stock market investing. Toward the latter part of my career, I started doing spiritual research after seeing a TV series about how psychics aid law enforcement in apprehending criminals and finding missing persons. As I neared retirement, I started getting ideas about including all this information in a book that I self-published under the title *Manifesting Abundance: The Universal Key*.

I decided to test the abilities of a number of psychics by using myself as a subject and then to report my findings in the book. Around this time, interesting things started to happen for me. I might be looking for a quote to use in the book, and it would pop up on TV a week later. All kinds of things started happening in which good fortune was coming my way. As I had readings with the top psychics I selected, that was one of the things that came out. They were telling me angels, masters, and guides were helping me in a variety of ways. One of these talented people actually quoted the angels and said because I "listened and took action the manifestation time was amped up. Gratitude really works."

Some of the key things that have helped me apply gratitude in every situation have been acquiring spiritual knowledge through reading. The *Bible*, the *Quran*, Buddhist and Hindu teachings, near-death experiences, reincarnation, and more recently, *A Course in Miracles*, which is a communication from the spirit or soul of Jesus to a research psychologist in New York City between 1965 and 1972, all were helpful. (By the way, I was told by one of the top psychics that Jesus wanted me to introduce people to the course.) From these resources, I learned that God or Source or whatever you call it, has a plan and the plan is for our good. Everything happens for a reason and is meant for our learning.

One of the things people have asked me over the years is how I can have an attitude of gratitude even in the face of unwanted events. To illustrate, I will give some scenarios and address how and why I can take a certain attitude in a question and answer format.

Question: What if you lost your job and don't have any money saved?

Answer: I believe there is a reason for it. God intends all circumstances for good. I tell myself I will get another job soon. I might have to adjust my expenses, and I can do that. I take action by identifying any programs to help me, and I follow up to see if they will work for me. If I identify that I am lacking in job search skills or education and training, I can create a plan to acquire the desired training or make another plan that will work. I might pray, "Thank you God for this learning experience. Show me how it works out for my good. Show me what I need to do."

Question: What if loved ones die?

Answer: No one dies, life continues without end. The spirit or soul is still very much alive, and I will see them again. They are in a better place. Would I want to hold them back from going on to a better place? No, I would not. So I celebrate their life and therefore do not feel strong feelings of grief. If I am facing illness or death myself, it is the same process of thinking. I also think along the lines of my being here at the calling of the Almighty, Source, God, etc. If Source calls me to be in another state or dimension by transitioning out of this earthly body, so be it.

Question: What if you don't have enough money even though you are working?

Answer: I know there is a way to get and keep money, and it is my job to educate myself on how to do this. It is similar for getting jobs. In any case, I continue to have gratitude for what I have and try to better myself at the same time.

If you are feeling gratitude, it is almost impossible to be feeling a negative emotion at the same time. Staying in gratitude allows for your cells to be in a healthy state, which obviously allows for very good health. It also allows for better problem solving because a relaxed mind is more creative. It allows for your angels to have a more beneficial effect because you are in harmony with the universe, with your heart and mind in a calm state.

I've noticed as I applied gratitude to every situation, many times the circumstances changed in dramatic, miraculous ways. By using gratitude in this manner, it never fails. You have gratitude when things go the way you want, and you have gratitude when things do not go the way you originally wanted, and miraculous things may happen. Expect miracles.

Jim Del Vecchio, M.S., C.A.S. has authored the following books and DVDs: *Manifesting Abundance: The Universal Key, Jesus Speaks, A Spiritual Path To Prosperity: For Teens To Seniors,* and *Making 30% A Year In Stocks, Trading Secrets For Mutual Funds.* He has a Master's Degree and a Certificate of Advanced Study in Counseling Psychology and a Bachelor's in Business Administration with concentrations in Accounting and Marketing. He has received awards and accolades for his work in career development, stock market investing, and spiritual research. He has been on a spiritual path since an out of body experience while in intensive care when he was 23 years old. LearnToAttractAbundance.com.

Coping with Chronic Illness and the "Just World Hypothesis"

By Dr. Madeline Altabe

My psychotherapy clients often share their struggles coping with illness. They have been reminding me to write about illness coping for a while now. For many of them, the challenge of living with illness is more than the symptoms themselves: pain, fatigue, and unpredictability. It is the social impact of the illness that leads them to sadness, isolation, and hopelessness.

For example, let's imagine an individual, Thea, with chronic fatigue syndrome and migraines. At age 27, she is typically home on the weekends recovering from her workweek. Thea has friends who go clubbing and they often invite her to join in, but she has learned that it isn't worth the energy expenditure. One Sunday afternoon, Thea has the beginning of a migraine, takes medication, and goes to bed. The next morning, she is still somewhat "out of it" and struggles to get ready for work. She manages, but arrives at work 20 minutes late. Her boss comes to her cubicle and has a tirade about the irresponsibility of the younger generation, how they just party and don't care about their work. He tells her that if she continues to behave this way, she will not succeed at her job.

Poor Thea; now, in addition to not feeling well, she must manage anxiety about her job. She is acutely aware of how her reality — overcoming the obstacle of her illness to work — contrasts with how she is being perceived by her boss. Migraine symptoms or not, this is a tough interpersonal challenge.

Now let's look at the Just-World Hypothesis and see how an understanding of this human thought process can help Thea manage what is occurring at work. During the mid-part of the 20th century, there was much research taking place on the irrational nature of human thought. In general, we take a large number of short cuts when thinking and, as a result, we sometimes distort perception to regulate our emotional state. During this period, social psychologist

Melvin Lerner studied how people respond when interacting with victims–innocent people who experience negative events. Not surprisingly, most people are distressed to watch others suffer. The research showed something deeper: If observers can distort the facts to make the victim seem responsible for the suffering, their distress is relieved. For example, this blame-the-victim thought process is at the root of why rape victims have their hemlines scrutinized. As the research progressed, Lerner found that human beings actively work to maintain a sense of justice about the world, an understanding that good things come to good people and bad people are punished.

These thoughts help people cope with the unpredictability of life and, unfortunately, they do not lead people to feel compassion or justice when it comes to those who have been victimized by unforeseen circumstances. This includes attitudes toward the chronically ill, a growing population in the United States, according to research by the Milliken Institute.

So how can understanding the Just-World Hypothesis help Thea? The knowledge can help her avoid internalizing the negative feedback about her performance. After all, this was not an objective evaluation; this was her boss acting out of his own fears of vulnerability. If she does approach him to discuss her circumstances, she may be able to empower him to help her. Since the basis of the distortion is a fear of needless suffering, allowing someone to relieve suffering may hinder the distortion. She can say something like, "Can we strategize how I can best serve the company even with my illness? I really value being productive." Or: "If I was slow in the morning due to my illness, would it help if I stayed later or worked from home in the evening?"

It may seem odd to suggest that the "victim" needs to work to help the blamer cope better. However, if you think about it, Thea and those who live with chronic illness do have an advantage. They have experienced "when bad things happen to good people" and learned to live without a false sense of security.

Thea also can do some things to help herself feel better. First and foremost, she can avoid self-blame. Just-World distortions don't just affect how we perceive others; they also can hurt us and negatively impact how we see ourselves. One approach is to make the distinction between immanent justice and ultimate justice, a tool that comes from Lerner's research on reactions to severe illness. People who seek out an answer as to why a family member got cancer are engaging in a quest that leads to blame and pain. A believer in ultimate justice will cope better by focusing on thoughts like, "In the long run, we will find a cure and no one will have to suffer," or "Good meaning/value can come from this bad experience." Thea could remind herself that 30 years ago, people doubted that chronic fatigue syndrome was a real illness and, while there is still insensitivity, progress is being made.

Sometimes even that is not enough, and it may be better to accept the world as partially unjust. In those moments, perhaps it is best to focus on the justice that is at work in the world. Perhaps this is why stories of heroic altruism move so quickly through social media. More importantly, being an agent of justice can affirm a "just world." What if Thea gave an extra tip to the pregnant waitress at lunch? Perhaps she could create an e-petition for an environmental cause she feels strongly about. Maybe there are things Thea could offer to do in the workplace to make it more sensitive to disabled workers. These acts foster hope for a just world.

Thea has many challenges in coping with her illness. She must avoid self-blame for the illness and for the social consequences of the illness. She must find her sense of justice in the world and manage the blame that others place on her for her suffering. I like to say that justice should be a verb not a noun; it is an action towards others and a thought process of the mind. Thea can use her understanding of blame the victim beliefs to deflect the injustice of others. She can act justly in the choices she makes in her world. Most importantly, Thea can empower herself by treating herself "justly."

Devol, R. & Bedroussian (2007). An unhealthy America: The economic burden of chronic disease. Milliken Institute. Retrieved from www.milkeninstitute.org/healthreform/pdf/AnUnhealthyAmericaExecSumm.pdf

Montada, L. & Lerner, M.J. (Eds.) (1998). Responses to victimizations and belief in a just world. New York: Plenum Press.

Dr. Madeline Altabe, a psychologist in Tampa, FL, provides psychotherapy addressing wellness, body image and eating disorders. Her practice is designed around well- researched, evidence-based interventions. Dr. Altabe has also taught graduate psychology students for 15 years most recently as an adjunct instructor online for the University of the Rockies. She was actively involved with the Ophelia Project in the Tampa area, a school-based curriculum on violence prevention, self-esteem and positive peer relations, girls' health & leadership development. Dr. Altabe has co-authored books & articles to include: *Exacting Beauty: Theory, Assessment, and Treatment of Body Image* and *Body Image: A Handbook of Theory, Research and Clinical Practice.* Visit www.radianceconsult.com.

How I Went from Homeless to Living My Dreams

By Steve Harding

I recently realized that my present life is exactly what I had dreamed it one day would be. I am financially secure, I live where and in a home that I want, I am in the relationship of my dreams, and I have perfect health. I am living a peaceful, joyful, and fulfilled life—amazing! It truly is most amazing because exactly three years earlier—May 2011—I was homeless, living in a place that had no running water and no electricity. I had no food, no money, and most importantly, no way out—so I thought. I felt truly hopeless, trapped, and defeated! But I managed to turn it around and beat the odds, and I want to share the story of how I did it.

It boils down to two main techniques: **The first is acceptance of responsibility for your life. The second is to develop an "attitude of gratitude."** These two areas have other smaller steps contained in them, but this chapter will give you all you need to begin manifesting the life you desire. Any further details you desire will be made available to you if you only ask.

First, let's look at what it means to be responsible for your life. I can assure you that when I first found myself in the homeless situation I was angry! I was strong into the "blame game" and upset with all the people who had failed me or conspired to make me fail. These feelings literally consumed my thoughts for a period of time. The cause for my trouble was "out there!" I knew none of this was my doing. I would often look into the mirror and cry out, "How did I get here?"

Then one day I looked into the mirror and realized only one person was looking back at me and perhaps that person had some culpability in my situation. I then had to look into the mirror and ask a different question, "Why did I choose poverty?" This was without a doubt the most difficult moment of my homeless experience—it was my fault and I had to own that! But it was also the most wonderful moment because I now had access to the possibility of changing it.

The next question, and this one is a critical key in creating what you want in life, became: "What am I really responsible for?" It was not the real estate market crash, the state of the economy, or the price of gas. What I was responsible for was my reaction to those situations, and they were driven by my thoughts. There it was: I was responsible for my thoughts, and my thoughts create my reality!

As Earl Nightingale put it, "I become what I think about."

Wow, what an amazing concept! I can focus my thoughts on how I want my life to be and my circumstances will change to create that life. My circumstances changed to create where I am now because of my past thoughts. It was interesting that by opening up to this idea I could remember the types of thoughts I had when things began to "go bad." The defeat, the disappointment, the anger, and the self doubt I had about my future. It had become a downward spiral.

Now all I had to do was shift my thinking to what I wanted, and how wonderful that would be. I felt plenty of resistance and disbelief that this would work, but I knew in my heart that I was onto something—and what did I have to lose anyway? So I started concentrating and being present to the little voice in my head and what it was telling me. Whenever I heard negativity, I would switch to imagining something pleasant.

Then things began to happen: Unexpected income came into my life, the condo I wanted was available, and the owners were friends of mine. They allowed me to pay my rent in arrears for the first year and did not require a security deposit. My life just continued to get better. Each time I reached a goal I set another using my thoughts and then got excited about its arrival.

This brings us to the second category of having "an attitude of gratitude." Developing gratitude for what we have and what we are asking for is powerful because it instills emotion into our desires.

Emotion is a huge catalyst in the manifestation process; it is energy in motion and powers the engine that moves our thoughts into reality.

But what did I have to be grateful for; my life was in the bucket! Initially, I knew I wanted to live on the water in a beautiful condo and have plenty of money, but that was too big a stretch from where

I was. So I took a different route. I decided to think of something that was already in my life that I could feel gratitude for; this was something I could do.

I picked the facts that I had a roof over my head, I was not on the street or in a shelter, and that I was healthy. I would close my eyes each morning, each evening, and as many times as I could remember to do this during the day and feel total gratitude, like it was the blood running in my veins. Even though nothing changed immediately, I soon noticed I felt lighter, happier, and I even laughed sometimes.

As things did begin to improve, I found myself able to feel grateful for small things that had not yet appeared in my life and, sure enough, soon they would. This increased my confidence in the process. Today, I spend much of my time thinking of how I want my life to be, and I do gratitude exercises several times each day. It is an enjoyable experience that makes my days peaceful and fun.

Let me close with this. I hope these words will be a contribution to your life and bring you the same results they have brought to me. A glass seen as half empty when combined with thoughts of lack, disappointment, and anger will eventually result in a completely empty glass.

A glass seen as half full when viewed from abundance, joy, and gratitude will quickly result in a glass that is overflowing.

Steve Harding is a retired small business owner who found himself homeless in February of 2011. During the following 5 month period he learned the process or "formula" that he had lived to create that situation in his life. By using that knowledge he has created a life of prosperity and peace. "The pain of being homeless came not from the physical circumstances but from the hopeless feeling of not knowing how to change it."He is the owner of OYOG, Inc., (Own Your Own Greatness!) whose purpose is to share what Steve has learned with as many people as possible through public speaking and workshops. Visit his website at www.ownyourowngreatness.com. Steve is an award winning Toastmaster, a published author, and has been a guest on live radio.

Acceptance Is

By Zan Benham

It is said that "Peace begins with me!" In fact, it does because every opinion, every perception we have is ours alone. Surely what others think often influences us, and that is My Perception, my way of understanding, and my way of seeing the world! If I don't know something it does not exist for me. Perception is everything!

I have often thought that if I did not know the horrors of the war in the Middle East that it would not exist *for me.* Is it possible that our Critical Mass Consciousness helps create and hold these disruptions in place? Do these continual thoughts also create weather patterns and other natural disasters? Could it be: Fire our anger? Water our tears? Earthquakes an explosion from hatred and frustration?

It is said that Peace will come when we become the
peace we envision.

So begins this dissertation of an important truth as I perceive it to be. Hopefully you will agree with me, because by doing so, you will in great part set yourself free of the tribulations of the past.

Real Time is in Breath Time. Breath marks this moment "Now." All else is past, as in memory, or future, as in projection. Only Now is Real! **Be-ing** exists Now, and Consciousness of Deity (God) exists in each breath.

In this moment Now, you and I are here. It is where we are! We may say that we are unhappy with this present situation and that we wish things to be otherwise. We may say that we wish we could have done it differently! Still everything IS, AS IS.

That is, ISNESS! Once something is said or done we cannot go back. There is no way to undo what IS, and wanting to change it brings in great tension and resistance. Simply said, "WHAT IS, IS! BE HERE NOW!" Breathe.

Acceptance is helpful because it releases resistances and the longing it sometimes holds. Often, this longing becomes obsessing. We want to change the situation! The body tenses up, and we blame others and get angry at ourselves.

We get ourselves all tied up in a tizzy of knots sometimes, and with great frustration we point our finger and blame the "them." We blame others for our unhappiness, misery, relationships, and loss. Whenever we point that ole finger at someone, three point back at us! If I don't like something or someone, whose issue is it anyway? It's mine, of course! People do what they do! They are just being who they are. I am the one having issue when I critically point my finger at them! Each time I do this I victimize myself, and I increase my feelings of powerlessness. There is a saying, "It is all an inside job!"

Acceptance and letting go of resistance brings us into the "Is-ness" of things. We say, in effect to ourselves, "I am here now, in this moment, and this IS!" I may not like it! I may detest it! I may move from it, and I may forgive it. However, I cannot change it!

I am here now. This is where I AM. This may feel like a form of surrender, and it is good to be in this space. It is a space of empowerment in letting go of wanting to change or control anything. It releases the resistance in a desire to love the Is-ness, unconditionally. You'll find it at the end of the exhale of the breath. Hold it there in the silence of the moment. Feel it! **IT IS, AS IT IS!**

What is next anyway? What would I choose to see or imagine becoming? Can I virtually fill my vision? No one can change what has been done, but each of us CAN CHANGE what may come next by where we place our focus!

There is indeed a Critical Mass Consciousness, which is the sum total of the focus of the individuals on this planet. We are all related whether we wish to believe it or not! The laws of Cause and Effect and of Sow and Reap speak for themselves. The Law of Attraction basically says that you magnify what you focus on, even if you don't want it! In a way, we are praying all the time, and every thought lives on somewhere. Energy never dies. What goes around comes around. The greater the anger, fear, and pain, the more separation we experience from the Divine Power within us and, as a result, the legacy of our being partly Divine is challenged. Hu-Mans are "the breath of God in a dualistic ego-oriented mind/body!"

In this moment I accept the all that is Right Now. I breathe in and I breath out as I consciously release all that is blocking me, be it opinions, predispositions, habits, mindsets, or predilections. I release angst, the fear, the hate, and all images related to my separation from the ONE. I begin to understand that no one is to blame. All are behaving exactly the way they know to be. They are simply responding to their own truth at this moment. **That is, what is!** I cannot change anyone, only myself! That is ACCEPTANCE!

I can change my perception now, and all else will change. I am the determiner of my perceptions!

If I come into this moment having released myself from my desire to change, or make different a person, place, or thing, I can suddenly feel the freedom of this, my Choice. I can choose to hold the light and hopefulness for well-being and awakening to come, where nations and people focus on making the world better for all its children. I focus on me, my inner light and intentions and then move as best I know how, into the outer world.

I have come to understand that the Highest Good has that single polarity that recognizes itself as LOVE, a frequency fostering joy, light, health, and well-being. It also sees all things as GOOD and all in DIVINE PERFECTION. We too can find that space inside of ourselves in the breath.

ACCEPTANCE IS. Breathe in, breathe out. At the end of each exhale hold the breath and feel this singular moment in this pause. This in Now, it is where you are AT. It is where Be-ing Is; All reality Is and "God" Is. Try it, you will like it!

Rev. Zan Benham, Butterfly Deerwoman, is an interfaith New Thought minister. She has a private practice as Spiritual Counselor, Certified Hypnotist, Shamanic Practitioner, and Reiki Master Teacher. She integrates these modalities in her work to empower her clients to embrace their own divine gifts and powers for healing. Zan has been a student of Metaphysics for over 40 years and has been active in Native American healing circles for almost as long. She regularly facilitates shamanic journeys, sweat lodges, sacred circles, and drum circles. She leads Drum Making workshops and has the honor to be a Sacred Pipe Bearer. Visit www.woman-spirit.com.

Releasing Ego and Learning to Live from Spirit

By Jami Lin

Do you want to be right or do you want to be happy? It's one of my husband's favorite mantras, and it's among many words of wisdom he has shared with me over the past 29 years. Some time ago, I thought I was happy and I was experiencing great success. I taught all over the world, had my books flying off shelves, and every weekend I was off on another teaching adventure. I was having a blast, doing exactly what I wanted to do in life. However, while I was living in outward beauty, I was always questioning my inner balance. The artful, metaphysical sciences that I love and share no doubt were (and still are) an extension of me, yet they were not my identity. I questioned, "Who am I?"

As life flowed, my ego and I journeyed down an eight-year rabbit hole of self-inflicted turmoil. It started with trusting a webmaster who couldn't deliver my vision. No matter how deep my love, passion, and success emanated from Feng Shui and ColorAlchemy, it was still my identity and outward expression. My heart and spirit were broken (or so my ego trapped me in that illusion). In addition to all the sleepless nights and wasted energy, retrospectively, there is no doubt that I gave myself (over-the-heart) breast cancer. I questioned my essence and how to be happy even during life's challenges.

Then in 2013, with one cancer-free year a fleeting memory, my ego was attacked by another person. The incident damaged my livelihood and questioned my reputation— the emotional hurt and broken trust were very real. The injustice and personal attack were as tangible as the cancer, and through sleepless nights, I recognized my egoic illusion of *needing to be right* was repeating negative and destructive patterns within me. At that point, I made a decision that my Spirit was not going to die in seeking justice for what I believe to be fair and/or making sure that others are accountable.

The Journey of Understanding

I traveled to India and sat at the feet of a real-deal guru. I toiled over the right questions in hopes of getting a glimpse into life's mysteries. Ignoring the notes in my hand, SwamiJi spoke in Hindi-heavy, toothless

English. Having to listen with keen focus and great fascination, he spoke as if he read my mind—as if he was teaching my Feng Shui class—as I always include this simple explanation...

An east-facing House is hotter in the morning — with the sun rising in east.
A west-facing House is hotter in the afternoon — with the sun setting in the west.
Align with the consistent energies of Heaven and Earth
(specific to how your home is aligned and designed)
to LIVE Heaven of Earth.

SwamiJi spoke in galactic proportions, without earthly limitations. He asked, "What is east and west?" and "How do you determine *time* if you are standing somewhere in *space*?" Immediately, I *heard* his point... but did I *understand*?

With a twinkle in his eye, one that revealed the light of his soul, SwamiJi said, "I see you have questions for me." Immediately he filled the room with joyful laughter, and I couldn't help but laugh along with him through happy, aching cheeks. At that moment, I gratefully considered the metaphysics of the unseen.

My thoughts then turned to the secrets of ColorAlchemy (do-it-yourself color healing): Perception activates mindful consciousness through the color sequence of rainbows (the vibrational science that differentiates color) and Ayurvedic chakra wisdom. When a rainbow magically appears, the universal ColorAlchemy of the mind pauses *Time*. As I learned through my years practicing interior design and Feng Shui, the alchemy of color (and a can of paint) instantly transforms *Space* too.

Even *Time* and *Space* are perceptions that may not be metaphysical reality.

"SwamiJi, I got it!"

So what does *"how I want to live"* depend on? Truth became so simple, I discovered a new reality beyond time and space.

I integrated my husband's wise words with SwamiJi's underlying message... *Do I want to be Right or Happy? Do I want to live in Ego or Spirit?*

Right = Ego / Spirit = Happy

Spirit isn't responsible for fixing what I perceive to be broken, especially at the price of breaking myself. The essence of Spirit is the accountability of being happy, maintaining honor, integrity and *BEing* authentic with a kind heart...and THAT is enough. THAT is my identity...in ALL Space and Time.

Om Tat Sat/Soham
in the **Absolute Truth Circle**
I Am That, I Am, That I Am, That/You are the same as I am

You hurt me, I hurt you? No, you are the same as I. Let's LOVE the same in THAT sacred place.

Sure, I will continue practicing singer John Mellencamp's powerful message, "You gotta stand for something or fall for anything," and I invite you to do the same. Sometimes ego provides the necessary courage to be a ripple for positive change. Do what you can do while holding Spirit close. Let your voice be heard...and listen when your heart says, THAT is enough.

Perhaps, within Spiritual joy, your reflection (the essence that you emanate) may be a stepping stone to help fix what is broken merely through living by example. Re-spin the cycle...I love you. Can you love me?

Why does the concern, *if you love me*, even matter? Living in wait, want, and wonder are thoughts of egoic illusions that block happiness. Let it go...Spirit doesn't care. Spirit wants you to Be Joy and to Live in the Present. Your Soul Essence IS Happy, why waste THAT by allowing your ego to be in control of... well, NOTHING.

Even though I am grateful to improve the lives of thousands of people through Feng Shui and ColorAlchemy, still being human, I experienced great internal battles and life-altering health issues in order to self-actualize SwamiJi's greatest joy. Laughing in recognition false perceptions leading to personal evolution. I am honored to share the secrets with loving intention for you *to get to know your Spirit* faster than I did!

I believe love for self and respect for others are Spirit's primal manifestations. Other life priorities that assist Universal birthrights to happiness are: follow your passions, have purpose, consistently hold your dreams, be authentic to yourself and others, stand in integrity, play hard at work, work hard at play, never settle for anything less than your best, forgive yourself and others, always wake up with the intention of being better and happier than you were the day before, and walk (the talk) with a bounce in your step and smile on your face.

Jami Lin is a world-renowned Color Alchemist, Feng Shui master, designer, Anti-Aging, Skin Care specialist, educator and seeker. Jami's award-winning books and talents provide personal discovery for greater love, success, and wellness for Inner Balance and Outer Beauty. Enjoy her Healthy-Life.net radio show and archives. Visit JamiLin.com for hundreds of complimentary, enlightening offerings. Make 20% on Jami's Organic Age-Reversing SkinCare, Chakra/Color products, and Feng Shui Interior Design / House Astrology with no-inventory, free web affiliation on SharingTransformations.com.

SECTION III:
SELF EMPOWERMENT

Outgrowing My Oppression

By Victoria Hawkins

Have you ever had the experience of observing another person, thinking, *"That used to be me!"* It is a knowing that the very vibration of what you are seeing matches an old way for you. I had this occur on a trip to India, and it allowed me to appreciate becoming the Me that I am meant to Be.

When I set out on this journey, I read about what to do as a woman visiting India: remain covered on my top, wear a ring to indicate I am married, and dress in the garments akin to women of the land. So I packed scarves to cover up. I wore a ring on my left finger, even though I am not married. Then I began to go into a hole; I felt fearful and pressed down. My vibrant self was draining out each time I covered up to walk outside or a man questioned my marital status. I suddenly knew that these travel suggestions were coming from a place of fear, but I had seen them as Truth I must follow.

One week into the trip, and I felt weighed down and suffocated. The heaviness of the words that I heard were in such contrast to the Namaste that floated on the next breath. We see God in everything, but then we categorize people into castes, and call some of them Untouchables. Where is the Love?

But then, where is my Love? Do I really sit before a man and see the Light inside of him, or do I sit in fear and eventually anger? When I see the light in the face of the homeless refugee child, can I also see the light in the man who skillfully refuses to serve me until another man asks for a meal on my behalf?

I knew I had a choice: Join in and feel the heavy blanket of oppression or be the Love I came to be? That day I made the conscious choice to see all of it, the oppressed and the oppressors with the Divine Eyes of Love. That was the beautiful moment where I felt the lift. I chose to be the light and allow myself to be the vessel of love that sees the beauty in both sides of the coin. I found the high vibration again; my experience shifted.

After that point, I realized that no matter where I am standing—whether on American soil where I know "the rules" or in a faraway place where I know nothing of the societal norms—I must be me. As I launched into the second half of my trip, I chose to wear scarves because I felt beautiful in them. I no longer shied away from questions about my marital status. I just answered them with a smile. I was just me, showing up in my integrity free of the baggage of oppression and fear.

Releasing the Past

Growing up I was my own worst oppressor, and by age 14, I was allowing others to determine my way of being. I chose boyfriends who abused me, I starved myself to be society's version of beautiful. I put constant pressure on myself to achieve. By 30, I was so lost from myself—and so used to relinquishing my power—that all I could "be" was what I thought someone else wanted me to "be." Until one day I woke up.

For me, it was like being in a dream that feels so real, but then starts to fade. For that briefest of moments you aren't quite sure which one is real, the dream or your reality. That was the way of my growth.

When oppression was my habit, I didn't realize that I was oppressing myself. I spent so much time looking for how to play by the "rules" that I couldn't hear my inner voice whispering to me, *"Are these rules still working for you???"* I began to grow, and that inner voice got louder, and the dream world began to look a little foggy. One day I asked the question out loud, "Is this really working for me?" The answer I heard back was a resounding "No." The shift was uncomfortable at first. Some days I would put the sleepy costume back on and some days I would rip it off exposing my True Self and my fears all in one fell swoop. Each time I let my True Self out in the open, I remembered that freedom. I remembered it from childhood, before I ever thought to let others control me.

Through the shift, I rediscovered mountain biking, and I rode trails near my home town of Brooksville, FL. One day a hot wind was blowing on me as I pedaled, and I imagined myself flying with the butterflies and the angels, and the thought hit me: *"I remember this. This is free."*

This is what it's like to wake up: It is a remembering. It is the little bits of life that spark something in your heart that says, *"This is who you are, I know who you are, follow me."*

> *We don't know we are oppressed until we realize we have a choice about being pushed down. Then we must recognize that we are in control and must make choices to change one by one.*

Just like a lotus in the mud, I took my time to find my beautiful. So many moments, and so many choices. The more I allowed myself to listen to that inner guidance, the more I faced my fears and grew in the process.

Our inner voice will always lead us to love, while our thinking mind will show us the way of fear. Today I ask myself this question regularly, **"Is it fear or is it love?"** It is my reminder to check in with what is motivating my choices. As I follow the voice of love, that deep knowing inside that I heard when I was a kid, I always flow in the direction of my best good. There is no oppression in love—no oppression of me or any other.

Outgrowing my oppression has allowed me to reconnect with the wisdom I knew when I was young. Today, I approach my life with the knowing that I can chose to be awake or asleep; fearful or full of love; free or imprisoned; living life or surviving it. I am always the one who holds my key.

Victoria Hawkins, LCSW, RYT has been enjoying being a voice in the world of health and wellness for many years. She is a Licensed Clinical Social Worker, adult and child yoga and bellydance instructor, meditation teacher, public speaker, intuitive artist and author/illustrator. She specializes in fusing art, movement, wisdom teachings, and yogic practice with intuitive guidance to create a unique way of connecting individuals and groups to their own inner voice. She attributes her insights and epiphanies to her commitment to deep listening to nature, the wisdom of children, unexpected teachers and her own Spirit Voice within. Visit www.victoriahawkins.com.

Metamorphosis: The True Story

By Natalie Amsden

When a caterpillar approaches its time of transformation, it begins to eat ravenously, consuming everything in sight. The caterpillar outgrows its own skin many times, until it is too bloated to move. It attaches itself upside-down to a branch and forms a chrysalis. This gentle encasing limits its freedom, yet protects it during the duration of the metamorphosis.

I can totally relate to this process. At one point in my life, I began ravenously consuming every inspirational book in sight. I felt heavy and as if I'd outgrown my life, yet I couldn't move. My world turned upside down. I felt like I was in a prison. Unbeknown to me, I was preparing for a period of personal transformation.

I had been living a stagnant life for a decade, dwelling in my comfort zone of detachment and security.

Everything was as I had always known. I'd been tolerating "chronic fatigue syndrome" for more than 10 years, so low energy was my norm. If you had asked me at the time I would have said I was happy, but isolation, self-sheltering, and denial can create that effect.

Don't get me wrong, I had some amazing times, and I spent a lot of time with family. Yet I woke up every morning to my alarm clock and contemplated all the evil things I would be willing to do if I would NEVER have to hear that damn thing again.

I loathed the whole working process. I felt like a voluntary slave. I had always told myself it was "what I HAD to do"—everyone else had to work too, after all. I had an empty, almost non-existent marriage, yet I was totally oblivious to it. I had convinced myself that feeling unfulfilled, lonely, and unloved was pretty "normal."

My conscious mind had submitted to a life of servitude and mediocrity, but my soul knew deeply that I was so much more.

My true self was conspiring to shift my reality. I didn't know what would come of me, but I let go and embraced my impending chrysalis.

There is a common misconception that once inside the cocoon, the caterpillar rearranges its parts and sprouts wings. The haunting truth is that if we were to open the cocoon halfway through the process, we would not find a caterpillar-butterfly hybrid, instead there would be a blob of goo. Within this ooze, a new type of cells referred to as "imaginal cells" begin to form, as if from thin air. They resonate at a different frequency, so different in fact that the caterpillar cells' immune system tries to gobble them up!

Eventually the imaginal cells become so numerous that they overpower the caterpillar cells. They draw together, forming clusters and feeding off the caterpillar soup in which they are growing. One day the imaginal cells collectively become conscious of what they are creating — an entirely new organism — and they begin taking on different roles and the butterfly begins to take form.

During my metamorphosis, my life disintegrated completely. Everything that no longer served me (which was nearly everything) began to fall away, rapidly. It was sticky and messy and at times I felt like I was being torn apart. However, at the same time I felt as if evolution had taken me over and I knew with every fiber of my being that I was on the right path. Within six months there was no trace of anything that had been in my life before. I walked away from my job, house, and belongings. I ended my marriage. I disconnected from people who drained me of life. I was unrecognizable and identity-less. I was neither bloated caterpillar nor emerging butterfly, just a blob of primordial ooze, ripe with infinite possibilities!

Each new spark of imagination and inspiration ignited a flame of knowing within me, an awareness that I was changing. As my vibration continued to increase, non-serving circumstances shifted away with greater speed, and I was drawn to live in alignment with my true self, my passions, my talents, and my longings with greater intensity.

When the butterfly has matured, the chrysalis becomes transparent. The butterfly emerges upside down and grasps its empty shell with such reverence, as if to say "thank you" to where it came from.

Suddenly things became clear to me. I was ready, and so I emerged back into the world, totally transformed.

> *I clung to the remnants for a little while, dangling there uncomfortably, in shock at who I had become.*

I was in awe and appreciation for all that I'd been through—

the emptiness, the depression, the numbness, the inspiration, the transmutation, and the reemerging. I didn't know what to do next, but I stretched my wings and trusted that when it was time, the wind would gently nudge me to let go and ride the currents of my new life. I was not afraid—nothing had ever felt so right.

I was authentically, totally, and emphatically ME for the first time in my life.

I took one last look back at all that I had been and then released it completely. I was blown away at how effortless it is to fly when you allow yourself to be who you truly are. Instantaneously everything I needed for my new life was drawn to me, one thing after another. A relationship that fulfilled my longing for true love and acted as a catalyst for my expansion entered my life, as did living environments within which I could get acquainted with my new self.

As I came into alignment with ME, I became aware that there was a larger transformation taking place. I became aware that I was like an imaginal cell within the chrysalis of our transforming world. I felt myself drawn to other imaginal cells, knowing that we all have a job to do—to follow what it is we feel most drawn to do and encourage others to do the same. For as we come together, we become catalysts for awakening.

Themes from this chapter were inspired by the book **Butterfly,** *by Norie Huddle.*

Natalie Rivera is a visionary speaker and entrepreneur. She is passionate about empowering others to GET REAL and live authentically. After a decade of living a life that wasn't hers and developing Chronic Fatigue Syndrome, Natalie let go of everything and completely transformed. Through her journey to healing she rediscovered her true self and greater purpose—to inspire others to transform their lives. Natalie "retired" from the rat race at 24, put herself through school as a freelance designer, created a non-profit teen center, and later created Transformation Services, Inc., which offers motivational speaking, curriculum development, life coaching, event management, and publishing. She is author of *Enlightened Relationships: Secrets to True Love and Happiness.* Visit www.joeelandnatalie.com.

Conscious Aging: Being Content With What Is

By Toni LaMotta

Our world is obsessed with youth and beauty. We are bombarded daily with ANTI-aging techniques and products. No wonder so many people fear growing older. Frankly, I'd rather not be ANTI anything but be FOR Aging…in a healthy and conscious fashion.

How would our world change if all of us began to see the aging process as a means of spiritual growth?

A few years ago I spent about three months in a hospital and nursing home. I noticed that I wasn't asking, *"Why is this happening to me?"* I wasn't feeling like a victim. I wasn't even asking, *"What did I do to cause this?"* as I might have several years previously. But, I found myself asking the question, *"What does my soul want here? What can I learn from this experience? What GIFT can I find here?"* I noticed that I began to see the aging process in a whole new way. Deep awakening was happening as I let myself just "accept what is."

The lesson was reinforced while visiting a dear friend 104 years young. She told me that she decided a while ago that it made no sense to complain because her life had gotten smaller (She had two rooms, which she seldom left, in an assisted living facility.) because if she were to be filled with complaints, she wouldn't be happy. She said boldly, "I'd rather be happy."

"Perhaps there are things I should be doing," she said. "Sometimes I find myself wishing I could go back to Sweden where I was born…but I know I will not be traveling anymore…so rather than wish I was doing what I can no longer do, I have learned to be SATISFIED with the fact that I HAVE done so much." (She and her husband were both pilots, so they travelled a great deal.)

I truly believe that the secret to her long life and happiness — besides having a bourbon and water each night! — is the fact that she is **CONTENT WITH WHAT IS.**

I'm not saying not to have wonderful memories. However, I have noticed that the unhappiest older people I know are those who long to be as they once were, rather than as they are now. Those who compare themselves with the way they were 20 years ago are engaging in an exercise certain to keep them in an unhappy state. One of the spiritual tasks of aging is learning to live without regret and striving to be happy with who and what we are right now.

I have noticed that whenever I am anxious it is because I am living in the future. When I let myself feel sad or depressed, it is because I am living in the past.

One of the things I teach as part of a program on conscious aging is how to do a life review. The purpose of this is both to see what we need to let go and also to find the seeds of possibility still waiting to be sown. Sometimes, when there are things we love but can no longer do, it's important to take time to recognize that it probably wasn't the particular THING that we want to do or have again, but the FEELING that came along with it that we yearn to experience. An exercise I teach people is to think about what they used to love about what they can no longer do; then find the feeling that they think is missing and ask HOW ELSE can I begin to experience that feeling NOW. It's a powerful spiritual practice!

The columnist Jan Glidewell once said, *"You can clutch the past so tightly to your chest that it leaves your arms too full to embrace the present."* Accepting what is probably is the MOST important of all spiritual practices. And certainly as we age, we get a lot of opportunity to practice that.

Every spiritual teaching emphasizes the importance of LIVING in the NOW. Letting go of the past can get very practical, and for me, spirituality is nothing if it is not practical.

I sold my home and moved into a smaller apartment not long ago. When I was moving, I found myself following the advice that was given to me years ago when I left California for Florida. The person helping me sort and pack would hold up everything before we packed it and say, **"Is this who you are today?"** I even let go of my doctoral dissertation because I realized that the learning is now inside of me and someone else could benefit from all those books and research materials. They are no longer serving me and are not part of my NOW. It also helped to clear up space on my bookshelves!

Most people, as they get older, begin to de-clutter and learn to live more simply. When we accumulate things, we are really telling the Universe that we don't trust that we'll have what we need when we need it. Or that we never think we have enough. The very search and need for more is often a denial of the depth and beauty of what is present at the moment.

A guru once asked his disciples what they would choose if they were offered $10 million or 10 children. Of course, most people shouted out, "*$10 million,*" to which he replied, "*You would be better off having 10 children, because then you wouldn't always be wanting more.*"

EVERYTHING in our lives can be an opportunity to complain, or an opportunity for spiritual growth. I know a woman, for example, who was recently diagnosed with macular degeneration... she calls it macular re-generation! She told me that the less she is able to physically see, the greater has been her spiritual knowing. As her eyesight has diminished, her INSIGHT is increasing.

Another friend, who is having trouble hearing, tells me that she is truly learning to LISTEN more carefully and to stay fully present to others as they speak.

The aging process offers each of us the exact experiences for our own growth and transformation. What are yours?

Dr. Toni LaMotta is a keynote speaker, best-selling author of *What You REALLY Want, Wants You* and spiritual teacher supporting people in growing spiritually through the process of aging consciously. She also helps coaches & speakers create, publish and market their books. Dr. Toni is also an expert in supporting people and organizations in reinventing themselves in midlife and beyond. Her experience? From Catholic nun, to computer programmer and dinner theater actress, to professional speaker, entrepreneur, and ordained New Thought Minister. You can read her blog at www.midlifemessages.com and find out more about her conscious aging programs at www.tonilamotta.com.

ALLOWING Transformation with the Power of ADVENTURE!

By Terez Hartmann

The Journey Really *IS* The Destination!

ADVENTURE and Transformation

All the preparations have been made — cast off the bowlines and sail away...

Isn't it amazing to see how well we live and how great we feel when we align with the spirit of fun and ADVENTURE?! The thrill of seeing, doing, or experiencing something fresh and new — particularly something you have deliberately chosen — is an ultra-fabulous way to get your juices flowing, reestablish your spiritual connection, and keep your life really rolling!

Considering that EVERY intention for change is linked to enjoying the journey more, while expanding your life and SELF, it's no wonder that participating in ADVENTURE feels SOOO tremendous! Have you noticed that when you travel to a place you have never been, try a new food or beverage, meet new people, hike a new trail, etc., all your senses become heightened, and you are much more present and alive? During these times, it is natural and easy to focus on beauty and fun — and appreciation always leads to a great destination!

ADVENTURE brings focus, presence, beauty, and appreciation along for the ride: Talk about one HECK of an A-List Power Tool for LETTING Transformation happen!

Embracing ADVENTURE means getting to ENJOY the journey NOW

Here's another great reason to embrace and incorporate The Power of ADVENTURE into your Transformation repertoire: Participating in some kind of happy ADVENTURE today and NOW allows you to ENJOY now, which IS what having new stuff/experiences is ALL about any way!

...Plus during the time you are consciously enjoying your adventure, you are too busy to be worrying about what hasn't happened yet, and shift from a mode of resistance to a flow of ALLOWING!

Think about it this way: When you discover you have lost something and then frantically search to find it, you rarely (if ever) do. In contrast, when you step away for a while to do something completely unrelated (which shifts your vibe and emotional state), lo and behold — and often right in front of you — you happen upon THE item you were once desperately searching for. This can also be the case for your DREAMS, VISIONS, and INTENTIONS!

At the same time, when you get into the groove of choosing to enjoy your day-to-day life and discover/create happy adventures just for the FUN of it — without any ulterior motive — you begin to realize that you no longer need some "future" thing in order to feel or truly BE successful. And then your great ADVENTURE of life only becomes even more magical at every turn!

The Power of ADVENTURE on YOUR terms

Like the word "success," everyone has her or his own idea of what ADVENTURE means. From simply choosing a new nail polish color or attending a different sporting event, to traveling solo overseas or hiking across the country, there's a level of ADVENTURE to suit every taste. Regardless of what others may deem to be a worthy ADVENTURE, all that matters in the grand scheme of Allowing YOUR Transformation is what gives YOU a sense of joy in exploring something new that appeals to YOU. Always remember this is YOUR Transformation and YOUR life we're talking about, baby!

Tools for the trip!

Find ADVENTURE in Your Own Backyard!

Even ordinary, day-to-day life can hold adventures, if you allow them!

1. Make a list of things you could do to add a sense of ADVENTURE and fun to your day-to-day life.

2. Keep this list handy (via posting it on your fridge, keeping it on your phone/iPad, or in your wallet) and choose at least one adventure weekly, daily or ANY time you'd like to add more FUN to your life!

Embrace ADVENTURE on a Larger Scale

When you wait to live, you live to wait, so why not start enjoying the journey NOW?!

1. Think BIG and make a list of the grander adventures you'd like to participate in that could rock your world in beautiful ways!

2. Choose something from your list, live that adventure, and enjoy the journey NOW!

The Bottom Line on Allowing Transformation with the Power of ADVENTURE!

Could you imagine what your life would feel like if you decided to find the fun, beauty, and freshness in ALL that you do every day and, as the icing on the cake, actually let yourself take that trip, start that business, plant that garden, invite new friends into your life, etc.?

What if instead of living solely for "destination fixation," being "forced" to change, or suffering your way from one point to the next, you allowed yourself to take the scenic route with the intention of exploring and savoring the sweetness of every mile and moment?

What if life felt more like a continuous flow from one awesome ADVENTURE to the next filled with bonuses, upgrades, and happy surprises with only small rest periods in between?

What if YOU truly ARE the Creator of YOUR life experience, the journey really IS the destination, and YOU are the one who determines whether Transformation is a rough ride or a JOY ride?!

Welcome to the destination and ongoing ADVENURE of LIFE!

"...Today I experience the greatest adventure of my life! I move forward with confidence, following the stars in my sky, for I know that where I go and where I am, is always, always right..."
---from "Being the Destination"
© 2004-13 T.T.R.H.

Terez Hartman is the author of *Allowing Your Success!*, a professional Keynote Speaker/Workshop Facilitator, Singer-Songwriter/Recording Artist, "Allowing Adventures!" & "Savor Vacation" Facilitator, true Renaissance Woman, and Visionary. She has spent the majority of her life working with the Law of Attraction and "Allowing," and owes her many years of ever-increasing professional success, constant flow of creativity, vibrant health, extraordinary adventures, amazing relationships with "cream-of-the-crop" human beings and—what she feels to be her greatest allowing achievement—her extraordinary "soulmate" marriage, to truly practicing what she teaches in her writings, presentations, adventures and music. Visit: www.AllowingYourSuccess.com and www.AllowingAdventures.com.

Authenticity—Being Your True Self

By Jim Toole

Authenticity is choosing to express your truth with integrity. It is not an idea, concept, or thought. It is living based on what is real and right to you. It is being true to your Self and therefore being genuine in the world. Being authentic requires knowing your inner personal truth, the ideals and beliefs that shape your life, and your perception of the world around you.

Authenticity is not influenced by the circumstances or conditions of your life. An authentic expression is the reflection of your inner truth out into the world, therefore influencing those circumstances and conditions. Being you, holding nothing back, allows for all of who you are to show up and make the differences you seek in your life. Life doesn't make you; you make life what it is.

Your authentic truth is found in the stillness and silence within, free from the effects of the world around you and even your own perceptions of it. It is yours and yours alone, unaffected by your past, current circumstances, or your longings for your future. It is your belief about your Self, right here, right now.

It is your understanding of your Self. It is "under" what you "stand" for, and therefore the very foundation of who you are. Your understanding of the world begins with truly knowing your Self. The expression of what you know to be true for you originates from your core beliefs.

Being authentic does not mean meeting the expectations of those around you, the circumstances or situations you are involved in, or the world as you know it. Being authentic is recognizing, accepting, establishing, and being what you know to be true and real at the very core of your heart and soul. In order to truly be authentic you must choose to live inside out.

As a result, authenticity requires no external action or expression.

However, because most of us live in the "real world," not isolated from it, we still must bring who we know we are within into our lives and the world. As you offer who you are from your authentic truth, all of your endeavors and interactions will be filled with your true essence and will be experienced by others to the degree that you are true to your integrity.

Integrity is the balanced union of your truth and your expression.
Authenticity is the balanced expression of your integrity.

Being authentic is natural and effortless. It requires no effort because it is the open expression of your Truth with a capital T. There is no how or why in being authentic. There is no right way to do it, only being you just as you are. There is no why because it is not about a reason; it is beyond the mind. It is being you without thinking.

Practical Advice

A good way to begin getting in touch with what is True for you is to stop, look, and listen. Stopping means taking a step back from everything in your life enough to truly be alone with your Self. Let go of what is or isn't happening, what needs to be done, or where you think you need to be, and become still.

The "looking" I'm speaking about is done with your eyes closed. To "see" your truth does not require the physical eyes; it requires your insight. After stopping and becoming still, begin to look within at your heart's true desires and your deepest personal longings. Look beyond what you "want" and get in touch with what really matters to you.

Listen for the whispers that are always occurring within you, which are usually drowned out by everything going on around you. Let your thoughts and even your feelings quiet. Listen to the dreams and wishes you have put away because of "the way life is." Listen carefully because no one else can tell you what your Truth is.

In order to make this process seem more practical and tangible, it is good to write some of it down. A simple idea to make it more specific is to pick five words that you feel best describe you and make note of them. If you want to see what the world thinks of you, choose someone you trust and ask that person for the five words he or she believes best describe you. This will help you get a different view of you. You can also work with each word, one at a time, to get

84

to know your Self better.

As you begin to recognize your own personal, intimate, and vulnerable truth, embrace it as yours and hold it close. As you feel yourself begin to claim it, let it embrace you. Surrender to it, and allow its influence to touch upon every aspect of you. Be with this truth in whatever way necessary to allow for it to penetrate into your thought process, your feeling nature, and your decision making. This will begin to establish your truth as your belief system about your Self.

As you begin to look out into the world from this renewed sense of Self, it will look and feel very different. As you begin to step out into your life being your Truth, everything you encounter, your activities, and your interactions will be changed by your new way of being. By continuing to live in this manner, your experience within your life, and your relationship with the world will be authentic. By being true to your Self, living with integrity and **Authenticity,** you are **Being Your True Self**.

Jim Toole is an inspirational speaker, personal and spiritual development counselor, workshop facilitator, meditation leader, teacher, and holistic healer. He has devoted over 35 years to working with people in their exploration and discovery of their own truth, purpose, and pathway in life. His intuitive guidance, meditations, energetic healing, writing, public speaking, and workshops have assisted and supported many in their healing, transformation, and personal and spiritual growth. His extensive training, certifications, and experience feed his dedication to bringing inspiration, wellness, peace, joy, harmony, balance and understanding to others through his 501(c)(3) nonprofit inspiration and wellness center, Radiance of Sarasota. Visit www.RadianceofSarasota.com.

Rolling with Life's Punches

By Maggie Webber

In mid April 1997, I finished my studies with Dr. Deepak Chopra, to become the Chopra Centre's first Meditation Practitioner in the Pacific Rim. I received so many benefits from learning this practice myself that I wanted to share its many gifts with other people. This desire became reality within less than a week of qualifying to teach it, when I was asked to share a stage with Deepak at the Entertainment Centre in Sydney, Australia, in front of an audience of over 2,500! That night was a turning point in my life.

For years I had been focusing all my time and energy on my former husband's career, which kept us bouncing between the United States, Europe and Australia. After I enthusiastically shared my experience with the audience and spoke from my heart, more than 450 people came up at the break and wanted to study with me. I had nothing to start a business, but I immediately knew that when you shift from "What's in it for me?" to "How can I serve?" the Universe will support you.

The realization that it was time to come out of my husband's shadow hit me hard that night. Our relationship was a total charade, and it was costing me my self-esteem. Worse, I wasn't living according to my soul's purpose. Four days after my epiphany, I asked for a divorce. I knew it was not going to be easy, especially with two little ones, no family or any real friends close by, and now no job either because—even though I had three university degrees and my own business—I had put my dreams and aspirations on hold to travel with and support my husband.

As I was the one who had chosen to go, my husband informed me I needed to find a new home! But as one learns when one begins to meditate, it is not what happens to you in life that is really relevant; it is what you learn from it and how quickly you recover.

The synchronicity in your life also picks up pace, so the day the kids and I had to leave our plush home was also the day one of my meditation students was leaving for England, and we were able to move straight into her little two-bedroom, furnished flat. One door closes, a better window opens.

Having learned from a father I rarely saw, I vowed that I would be there to watch my children's sports on the weekend, volunteer at their school canteens, read to them each night and go on at least one holiday together each year, even if it was an inexpensive one. So I did my utmost to find a way to work from home, so I could take them to school and be there when they came home. I had seen so many latchkey children becoming troubled. So I worked my meditation seminars into their father's schedule, which meant he saw them one weekend every five. I jumped into network marketing and did some public speaking, too. Both things I could do around my very talented children and their sports, drama, and many other interests.

Getting Back in the Ring

Then I discovered property investing. I started with one investment property, and then added another and another. I turned these into short-term rentals and ran a business online where I took bookings from overseas. Then I got over-confident, and I tackled a $6.5-million property development, where I was due to make $800,000 profit. But my financier went belly-up, the market turned, and I now couldn't settle on two unbuilt properties I had put a deposit on. So "boom" — I lost $100,000 overnight. I had the option of going bankrupt, as did every other member of my investment group. But there was part of me that could not take the easy way out. I felt I had to pay back my creditors, no matter how long it took.

Interest added to interest, and financially I was going backwards by the day! I couldn't sleep, gained weight, became a recluse, was too ashamed to ask for help from my family and, even though I was meditating each day, I developed depression. I found a life coaching course online, where we paired up with a buddy and kept each other accountable. This was all I could afford at this stage. Still, it was a great start. Very quickly I got my life got back on track. I saw the incredible power of having a coach and being accountable to someone else. It was a simple three-month program and I was close to finishing it, feeling like a completely new person in just 10 weeks. My income had more than doubled, my sleep issues had disappeared and my weight had dropped. I was feeling happier and more fulfilled than I had in years.

One of my property investing friends—who had chosen to go bankrupt and assured me that she had found such peace by doing so—became a financial planner. Ironically, she looked so well and happy, whereas I was working harder and going further backwards. I was due to meet her for coffee, when I got the call from her former boyfriend—"please come to Cherie's funeral." She had gassed herself, leaving behind two little boys aged ten and eight. At her funeral, we gave her a standing ovation. Finally, the recognition this talented and marvellous, yet troubled, woman had been crying out for all her career. Too little, way too late.

At her wake, as coloured balloons disappeared into the cloudless blue sky—each showing one of her gifts, values, hopes and dreams—I decided that NOTHING was ever that bad to end my life over. I signed up for a course to become a Life and Small Business Coach the following week, and have since become a Master Coach. For the last few years, I have made sure I will not die with one note of my music still in me—and neither will anyone I coach!

I am sure life still has plenty of surprises in store for me, and not all of them will be pleasant. Nevertheless, there is one thing for sure. My experience in life so far has taught me to dodge many an uppercut and right hook, and if one does connect, I now have the strength, courage and resilience to take it on the chin, learn the lesson from it and get back in life's ring for another round.

Maggie Webber, from Hobart, Tasmania, has has 35 years of experience providing individuals and corporations tools to increase productivity, manage stress levels and achieve a greater work/life balance. Her list of clients includes professional athletes, top executives and world renowned entertainers. After receiving a Bachelor of Education and Business Leadership and a Master of Commerce, she became Dr. Deepak Chopra's first certified meditation practitioner for the Pacific Rim. Using her NLP and Life Coaching certifications, she created her '3 Months to Transformation' program, to help her clients identify their true passions and break their life goals down into bite sized and attainable pieces. Visit healthywealthywisegroup.com or shifthappensnow.com.au.

Removing "The Box": Learning to Think Like a Child

By Darcey Pollard

We all know that "thinking outside the box" means to find another option or solution. At times this can be challenging, whether we are searching for a solution to a new problem at work, moving through a personal struggle or trying to change something within our life. Solutions don't always come easily, so I went in search of a simpler and more effective way to find them.

My mission was to find someone to model who could teach me how to instantly, on-demand, think outside the box so that, along with taking action, a solution would be inevitable. To do this I knew that I needed to find the answer to three questions.

- Who excels at this kind of thinking?
- How does this person do what they do?
- How can I replicate this to achieve similar results?

I began exploring my library and speaking to the most successful people I knew to find out what they all had in common when overcoming adversity and challenge. It turns out that at one time we all had this ability, and it developed in childhood. In fact, I found that kids are the best when it comes to this kind of "instant-solution" thinking. Any parent can tell you that if you ask children any question, they will quickly have an answer for you. Whether that answer is right or wrong is irrelevant as we are searching for ways to generate options because any answer can be a preliminary option.

My focus then turned to the next question, "How do kids do this?" How is it that children have this amazing ability to always come up with a plethora of options, and when they grow into adults they seem to lose this ability? The answer seemed to be two-fold.

First: Children are not as worried about being criticized, judged, or dismissed for their answers in the same fashion as adults. In today's society, adults have a fear of being judged by the people around them and, even worse, to be completely dismissed as being wrong. People just go on without saying anything, rather than risk being made to look foolish.

Second: Although children filter their world in relatively the same way as adults, they tend to believe that more is possible because they've had fewer setbacks and therefore are somewhat more optimistic about possibilities. Within our brains, we all use the same groups to sort information including memories, attitudes, values and beliefs, rules about time/space/matter/energy, language, rules around how we process information and references to decisions we've made. The differences between adults and children lie in what information is important to them, what they believe or distrust and, most important in this context, their evidence base of what is possible.

Dare to Dream

Both of these factors affect how big people dare to dream and how likely they are to achieve those goals. With an understanding of how they do what they do, we need to distill the information a little more and work out how we can replicate and apply it to our lives. We know that we have internal filters that narrow down our focus of the world around us based on what we include within them; children's filters are broader as they take in all that they can with nothing being irrelevant to their learning. Adults are narrower, as our learning tends to be more specific. We take on a certain curriculum at school, move into a particular career path and gain more focused information from varying arenas throughout life such as the Internet, media outlets, schools, institutions and religious, social and cultural groups. It is a natural progression, and it is how we master certain skills.

To help broaden our focus to devise more possible solutions, there are three things that we can begin to do today to temporarily step out of our narrowed filters to allow us to dream bigger and come up with possible solutions to any problem almost instantly.

Ask great quality questions. The quality of the questions that you ask yourself is a direct reflection of the success you can achieve and how well you can broaden your focus and come up with solutions. For example, instead of asking, "What do I want from life?" ask, "If money was no object and nothing could stand in my way, what would give me an even more fulfilling life?" Same question, different grade.

Get curious. Children are naturally inquisitive. They are constantly learning about their world and are always trying to work out *why* and *how* things are. Being curious gets us to explore ideas and concepts that we would otherwise have dismissed as not being relevant. Ideas breed other ideas.

Model. When toddlers look to acquire new skills and to belong, they model their parents. Likewise, teenagers model their favorite celebrities. If you have a problem, I can assure you that you weren't the first, and you can simply seek out somebody who has successfully overcome the problem or who has achieved the outcome that you want, and then model what they did. Simply: find the person, find out how they did it, and then find a way to adapt and apply it to your life.

It is all too easy to forget what is possible in life. We put blinders on, just go with what we know and, when faced with a problem that seems comparable to the size of Mt. Everest, we get overwhelmed and don't believe we have the skill or prowess to handle it. By taking a step back and thinking as our younger selves would do, we have a unique opportunity to take a fresh look at our lives and come up with solutions to seemingly impossible problems that we never before thought conceivable.

You have it all within you right now to remove "The Box!"

Darcey Pollard is a success strategist based in Melbourne, Australia who has helped clients internationally achieve new levels of success in both their personal and professional lives. He also works with business' to improve team productivity, communication, and leadership skills. A person who holds high expectations for both himself and his clients, Darcey is constantly seeking those that are "doing it better" so that he can then learn their principles of success and put these into a system everybody can use. Darcey can be contacted directly at darceypollard@gmail.com and through his website www.mrdarceycoaching.com

Getting IN TOUCH with Your True Self

By Dana Houk

It is important to discover who you really are or who you would like to become. As a life coach I love helping clients get IN TOUCH with their true Self. Ask yourself these powerful questions. What do you think is most important to you? Family? Friends? Having fun? Spirituality? Money? Intimacy? Health? Career? Being bold? Independent? Really think about these questions and write down what resonates with you most on this list. What do you think prevents you from having what you really want? Most people find that the answer is fear. While it is easy to stay within your comfort zone, I encourage you to challenge yourself and try something different each day.

When I asked myself those same questions, I found that it was hard for me to be bold in person. In the beginning, I am quiet and shy around people I do not know. I knew that I would need to overcome that trait to become a successful life coach. Ironically, I can speak with people I do not know for hours on a daily basis over the phone. Although I knew this was an issue for me, I was not sure what I would do about it. Then, I was given the opportunity to be bold. I was taking classes and assigned an interactive observation exercise. The assignment was to observe strangers and to make assumptions about them. Then, I had to ask them specific questions. Needless to say, I was apprehensive about the assignment.

The Assignment

A few days later, I went to a popular coffee shop alone, which I rarely do. As I was getting my drink, I noticed three businessmen sitting at a table with their laptops. There happened to be an empty chair right next to them. I thought about my assignment and knew this was my opportunity. I sat in the chair and listened to the three businessmen talk about their dogs. I was expecting to hear them talking about business. I had to talk to one of them, so I chose the closest man sitting next to me. Before I spoke to him, I tried to think about what he valued, what his dreams were, and what was important to him now. I thought of things such as family, money, and career.

As I was making my notes and trying to gain the courage to approach him, they were about to begin their business meeting. I knew I had to seize the moment, so I leaned over and asked if he would participate in my assignment. I told him I had three questions to ask him. I assumed he would say no because they were busy, but he was willing and very receptive. I asked him what he valued most. He answered his family. Then I asked about his dreams. He said he wants to see his kids be successful, and then everything else would fall into place. For my last question, I asked what was important to him now. He answered contentment. It took less than two minutes and I thanked him for his time.

I admit that I was nervous during the observation exercise, but it was not as scary as I thought it would be. In regards to the assumptions I made about the businessman, I only had one answer right (family) out of three.

It is human nature to assume what people are like based on what they look like or what they are doing in that moment. However, you never know what someone is really like until you speak with that individual.

This assignment tells a story about the fears I overcame, assumptions people make, and it allowed me to get IN TOUCH with my true Self — and you can do the same!

Everyone Has a Story

As you get IN TOUCH with your true Self think about the stories you possess. Does your story define you? Some people may argue that a story is just a story or that stories make us who we are today. Sometimes people can get stuck in their stories. There are many opinions about this subject, and none of them are right or wrong.

I believe there are two issues that can negatively impact stories. First, some people will try to change your story and how you perceive it. They may retell your story in such a way that they try to simplify it and what it means to you. Do not let anyone make you feel like your story does not matter.

The second biggest issue with stories is when people get "stuck" in their story. This can prevent them from moving forward. When certain things happen to individuals their mind tends to replay it over and over again like a broken record. Remember, beliefs create your reality. Cognitive therapy can help change those thoughts, behaviors, and triggers. However, therapy tends to focus on past issues. Although life coaches are not therapists, they can help clients reframe their thoughts from past events to future events. They can turn stories into something positive and meaningful. When people journal stories, talk about them, and work through those stories they can move forward.

When you are ready to make new stories just remember that people can be a part of your life, but it is your ink that writes the story.

Overcoming Fears and Putting Goals into Action

As a life coach, it is important to get personal with clients by asking potent questions. This may require them to dig deeper for answers. So, I am going to challenge you to overcome your fears and put your goals into action. Imagine what it would be like if ALL OR even some of your dreams came true. If NOTHING could stop you, what would you really want to do? Think about it, believe it, and achieve it. If you do not try, you will never know the outcome. One of my favorite quotes from Audrey Hepburn is, "Nothing is IMPOSSIBLE, the word itself says, 'I'm Possible!'"

Dana Houk holds a Master's Degree in Organizational Psychology and Development from Walden University. Dana owns and operates In Touch Coaching LLC, a business that specializes in Life, Career, and Relationship Coaching. She is also a certified Life and Peer Coach who works with an online university as an academic advisor/ success coach. She has spent over 1,000+ hours speaking with the hundreds of people she has coached. Dana is a solution-focused life coach who provides support and practical feedback. She helps clients achieve personal growth by integrating tailored coaching techniques. This allows individuals to get IN TOUCH with their true self! Visit www.intouchcoachingllc.com.

Letting Go of the Daily Grind

By Alexander Dolin

I have felt the daily grind and stress from having a job I loathed. For almost three years, I worked for a large freight corporation. As a dockworker, I had the responsibility of loading and unloading semi-trailers, often full of skids with freight, and sometimes full of equipment that had fallen off skids, such as tires, boxes and other items. Needless to say, this job and the environment were very demanding and stressful.

Each dockworker was constantly under pressure from management to do the job both quickly and accurately. The supervisors wanted us to stay productive and get the trailers unloaded quickly, but they also needed us to take our time and "do the job right the first time." Oftentimes, I felt torn by these demands: on one end they want me to speed up and finish unloading the trailers, but at the same time they want me to slow down and not damage the freight. The environment was chaotic, as there were almost 200 open semi-trailers and almost 50 other guys on forklifts working on the same dock at any given time. I tried to do my best work every day — to keep productivity up without harming the freight.

After I learned the best practices and the tricks of the trade, I gained more trust among my colleagues and the supervisors. In fact, the supervisors changed my role from just being an unloader to loading, too; I was now in charge of making sure that all of the freight in one section of the dock was loaded properly and timely. Throughout the evening, 30 other dockworkers brought freight that needed to be shipped in the trailers for which I was responsible. At times, the amount of freight and stress was overwhelming.

I honestly did not enjoy going to that job. The entire environment was negative, and almost all of my coworkers disliked the stressful environment. The day-to-day interactions among the employees were testament to this: the dock was filled with grumbling, complaining and aggression. Very few workers had a positive outlook, and it seemed like we could never please the managers or each other on the dock. Over time, I burned out and eventually quit the job.

I tell this story not to put down my fellow dockworkers or the company where I worked, but to relate my experience of living that daily grind. That dock was not a place of encouragement and hope. My memory serves as an avenue of empathy, so I can reach out and connect with others who are working in a stressful workplace.

Before I left the company, I did not comprehend that I was stressed out. I only knew that the job was not my passion. I was a part-time student, and I hoped it would not become my career; it was merely a source of income. In knew that after finishing my education, I would eventually move to a profession that better suited my purpose in life. I am blessed to have found that calling in stress management coaching and professional counseling.

The Serenity Prayer

If I could go back to that loading dock job with the coping skills I have today, I would not experience that same high level of stress. That said, I would like to share one of the simplest and most profound ways that you can combat stressful situations in your life and preserve your own peace of mind. It's called the Serenity Prayer, and anyone can use it to instill a mindset of hope that will help release stress. The Serenity Prayer is a simple yet powerful statement that was authored by the American theologian Reinhold Niebuhr (1892–1971). Today, it is used in many 12-step recovery programs, and it transcends religion (so if the word "God" doesn't resonate with your belief system, just remove it):

"God, grant me the serenity to accept the things I cannot change, courage to change the things I can, and the wisdom to know the difference."

This statement recognizes that there are many things outside of our control, and that we need to let go of them. We need to find peace within ourselves because we cannot control the actions and thoughts of others. However, we can learn to control our own thoughts and actions, and we need courage to do the best that we can do on a personal level. And when there are situations where we find ourselves unsure if there is anything we can do, we need wisdom to decide if we can or should act with courage or simply let go.

Let peace flood in when you realize that things are out of your power.

If I had this influential mindset when I worked on the loading dock, I might have lasted longer in that position, perhaps until I graduated. I would have realized what was in my power, loading the best trailers on the dock, and focused on that task. I would have been able to let go of the things I couldn't control, such as the mistakes that other dock workers made. I would have had the wisdom to know that fixing their mistakes was part of my job, and I could have released the pressure I felt from the extra time it took to do this. I would not have buckled under the pressure managers placed on my shoulders and their constant hounding to get the job done faster.

It's a blessing to learn from the mistakes of others — in this case mine! The next time a flood of pressure or stress comes rushing in, quickly remind yourself of what is in your control and what is not, and remember to say the Serenity Prayer.

Alexandar Dolin is a Board Certified Advanced Christian Life Coach through the International Christian Coaching Association (ICCA). He is the Founder of Fully Alive Life Coaching and a Christian Stress Management and Self-Care Life Coach. Alex is also a Counselor-in-Training in the State of Ohio as well as a Biblical Studies Professor with Ohio Christian University. In his free time, he enjoys playing music. He plays guitar, bass, mandolin, banjo and drums. Alex also enjoys exercising and baking and in his free time, Alex volunteers with Kiaros prison ministry and at his church. Visit AlexanderDolin.com.

SECTION IV:
HEALTH AND HEALING

Heaven's Heart Medicine:
Healing from the Loss of a Beloved Pet

By Sylvia Edmonds

It was an achingly cold fall day in 1998, unusual for southwest Florida. With a matching ache in my heart, I frog-marched myself into the leaf-strewn yard and began raking ferociously. This ferocity was an old coping habit of mine, one I used to force myself through a demanding task to diminish the impact of a pain.

Several weeks earlier, my old doggie soul mate, Rachel, had passed over and I was in deep, raw grief. My heart hurt so bad it was threatening to close down. I worried for my sanity. How could I still feel life so much when my little companion was no longer next to me? In the moment of pausing to reflect, a gentle, familiar, soundless Voice whispered up from within, "What would it take to open up your heart?"

It stopped me in my tracks. What? Is that really what I wanted? To open up for even more pain and sorrow? Hey, Voice, I'm still bleeding for Rachel here!

The Voice persisted, "What would it take?"

Grieving seemed to me something like a Ping Pong game, as uncontrollable forces played mercilessly with one's emotions. The heart was bounced crazily from searing pain to peaceful moments, from hot anger to the guilty joy of good memories.

I stopped still, plopped myself onto the low wall skirting the yard, leaned on the rake and breathed deeply.

"What would it take?"

That wise-guy Voice proceeded to startle me further by going ahead and answering its own question. Or was that my own tender heart responding? I wasn't sure, but somehow now it didn't matter.

"Baby animals." Where on earth DID that come from?

Visions of puppies, kittens, bunnies, fawns and nestlings began to kaleidoscope through my mind's eye, and a tiny smile made a tiny crack in my scared and crazy heart. I felt my body soften and relax. Some kind of magic was infiltrating the Ping Pong game.

"Good answer, Self," I murmured. (Or whoever you are.)

Strangely lighter in spirit, I resumed raking and forgot all about the dialogue. The refuse I was cleaning up became the center of a new mindful focus, and my body felt good to be useful. For the moment, my mental health was salvaged and my ferocity softened. The Ping Pong ball had bounced into a healing zone, an intermission in the crazy, grief game.

Within the hour, I felt normal enough to venture out on a mundane task, without needing that ruthless frog-march. I drove a few miles downtown to the ATM machine and completed a routine transaction. Exiting the small ATM room attached to the credit union, I nearly tripped over a medium-sized cardboard box. Surely, it had not been there when I arrived, and I had not seen anyone moving around outside. I was mildly irritated for losing my balance and was tempted to kick it aside and keep going.

But, an invisible inner force stopped my foot in mid kick. "You are meant to find this box," was what it said without a voice. Gingerly, I knelt down, opened the box flaps, expecting nothing and found myself gasping. My eyes lit upon a tiny baby squirrel nestled in the corner, bright eyes open wide. It looked healthy but was clearly abandoned and alone.

Imagine what my heart did at that moment! The Ping Pong game vanished altogether, and a chuckle bubbled up from the depths of my belly. Ah, the cosmic irony of this moment, in light of my erstwhile dialogue back there in the yard. My achy-breaky heart had just been handed the medicine so skillfully prescribed!

"Baby animals, indeed," I said to myself.

Picking up the box and its wee resident, I headed for the car. I knew what I had to do: deliver my precious cargo and me to the Pelican Man's Bird Sanctuary in Sarasota, FL, which also takes in injured or abandoned wild animals. They nurtured, healed, housed and/or released their charges as soon as possible.

This baby was not for me to keep, I knew in my heart and soul, but it was mine to hold for a bit and to shepherd into its new future. Although my time with Rachel had been so much longer, I was struck with the realization that it was truly a similar mission: to hold, to care for, and then to release with love. I wondered if this furry little visitor also knew that it had come to perform a mission for me. Someone knew. I knew.

During the car ride, the blossoming of my heart continued apace. As a gifted one-handed driver, I tenderly lifted the infant from the box and held it close to my heart. It snuggled right in, making itself perfectly at home. I melted some more. Speaking softly into its tiny shell ears, I stroked its silky baby head with my thumb.

"Oh, baby, thank you for coming today," I crooned. "I'll take care of you. I love you, little one." I was almost embarrassed by my own gushing emotions, but mercifully, it really didn't matter. The magic happening was all that mattered. Over and over, I whispered calm, soothing words, petting and kissing the velvety fur, feeling the rapid, little heartbeat. Glancing down, I saw the baby eyes close slowly into peaceful sleep.

There was no way that this divine message could escape me.

As I pulled into the sanctuary parking lot and stopped the car, I sat still for a few more precious moments. I savored the miracle of oneness, of true healing, of answered prayer. Then it was time. Holding the baby close and secure, I rang the bell and greeted the smiling volunteer.

"You'll love this one. It's an angel," and with a smile of my own, I surrendered the baby.

My drive home was graced with the dazzling spectacle of dancing sunlight on Sarasota's turquoise bay. Resting my hand on my freshly opened, happy heart, I breathed in the essence of beauty. An infant's smile of innocence crept fully over my face, and I was totally filled with gratitude. Now, I felt connected with my own strong heartbeat, the baby squirrel's phantom heartbeat and, wonder of wonders, the feeling of Rachel's dear heavenly heartbeat next to mine. All as one.

My soul knew for sure it would ever be so. Heaven's heart medicine is like that.

Sylvia Edmonds was born and raised in a small Ontario town where she learned early to love nature. Also loving the mystical side of life, the power of words and heartfelt connections, she brings these gifts together in her healing work. Focused on relations between animals and two-leggeds, she offers touch therapies, pet loss grief counseling and story-telling. Through her decades of experience as a counselor, friend and seeker, she shares her gentle humor, her understanding, a tender touch and an invitation to expand and grow. Discover more by exploring Sylvia's website: www.touchforanimals.com.

Cooking on Faith:
A Culinary Spiritual Awakening

By Rachael J. Avery

Six years ago I awakened to a personal transformation tool that completely sculpted my life. In 2008 I was 60 pounds overweight, had a negative bank account, a foreclosure on my home, an abusive relationship that defined me, had just received my second job layoff, and a severe manic depression episode laid me out on the couch for three months straight. Hope had officially left the building.

I felt defeated, and I began the process of taking my own life. As my soul began to leave my body, a powerful inner voice I'd never heard before said, with thunder, "Get up! Get up! Get up! I am not done with you yet."

Hearing that higher inner voice for the first time terrified me. I crawled up the wall with my back, bandaging my own wounds, and began stumbling down the hall.

"Where do you want me to go?" I screamed from the pit of my stomach. "I have nowhere to go and nothing to live for!"

Before I became anymore confused, the once-forceful higher voice fell soft and gentle. I found my two feet planted in my kitchen. Before I could even ask what I was doing here—I had a near-empty pantry and fridge, and I was almost empty of life myself—that now-gentle voice sighed and simply whispered in my ear, "I want you to create something from nothing my dear."

I didn't have the energy to agree or disagree. I found myself grabbing a pan and cooking on pure faith, not even having the energy to wonder what it was I was making. What came of my culinary spiritual awakening was a vegetarian Mexican casserole dish that I have not been able to repeat to this day. I had never created something so beautiful, nourishing, and authentic from so few resources! This heightened level of creativity, talent, and power could not be explained, but it has grown exponentially along with me in the kitchen ever since.

Putting off major life changes can be easy. Excuses prevail as to why we aren't juicing kale every day, prioritizing dance lessons over watching another episode of *Dancing With the Stars*, finding or pursuing that red-hot purpose beckoning to us. Life's distractions and our internal reasons to put life on hold can make us feel all too human at times. However, hope is just around the corner. As a matter of fact, it's just down the hallway.

Indeed, personal transformation is no further than your kitchen. Cooking is the most accessible, affordable, right-underneath-your-nose tool for empowering a life shift. How awesome is that?

Simply tuning into the frequency and intent of cooking, while knowing that it is a self-learning platform, is all you need to convert your kitchen into an episode worthy of Oprah's *Super Soul Sunday.*

Next time you hop in your kitchen, consider being an open channel to absorb five life lessons from cooking. They will give you access to your "easy button" for personal transformation and make your next meal time a "heal time" for your soul.

Five Life Lessons from Cooking

1. **Forgiveness**. Celebrate your next mistake in the kitchen! When you burn that garlic gluten-free bread with Earth Balance butter say, "Who wants Cajun croutons? They're as perfect as I am." Practicing the art of forgiveness in the kitchen and celebrating mistakes rids your life of guilt and shame.

2. **Creativity**. Try new things! See ingredients you already have with multiple purposes. Can you use a collard green leaf as a tortilla? Consider using your favorite organic jam as a sweetener for your own oil and vinegar dressing. Cook with the colors of the chakras in mind to keep those energy centers balanced. When we see what we have in a new light, with creativity, our resources expand exponentially.

3. **Get Grateful**. Do you really think the five-year-old, hard-as-a-rock garlic powder lingering in the corner of your spice pantry is really good? Clear the energy and increase vibrational flow by releasing what you no longer use. You can do this each time you cook. As you gain clarity and see what you have, you become grateful.

4. **Play**. Is there a reason why you're uptight in the kitchen? Release your clenched buttocks long enough to play some music, light a candle, and practice some of those *Dancing With the Stars* moves. Try singing "Cook-aroke" to spice up the atmosphere. Use playfulness to overcome the I'm-tired-don't-feel-like-cooking bad mood blues.

5. **Empty Yourself**. Empty your head and your heart before walking into the kitchen. Ask your guides to help empty limiting dinner beliefs that influence what type of cook you are, what you are capable or not capable of doing, or that you don't know what you're doing. When you empty yourself, you leave space for your Higher Inner Chef to come in and take

over and make you the most brilliant cook ever!

It was cooking for personal transformation that turned the worst day of my life into my sprout of personal power. I never meant for a vegetarian Mexican casserole to be a part of my soul's purpose, but we all get our callings in different ways.

Only months after beginning to build my intuitive culinary confidence and starting to cook differently on that drizzly day in 2008, I miraculously allowed forgiveness to flow into my heart. And with forgiveness, I began the journey of blessing and releasing 60 pounds from my physical body.

I used creativity to see my world differently and, as a result, I was able to leave an abusive relationship that spanned 13 years.

I became grateful by seeing my resources as abundant instead of seeing myself as a victim, and I started my own business.

I used my playful spirit to find my own true joy, and I was able to get off depression medications.

I fearlessly emptied my mind and started taking orders from my Higher Inner Chef to find peace.

Cooking for personal transformation isn't only focused on what you eat, it's also exploring how much you're willing to learn about yourself in a small, accessible, affordable space like your kitchen—whether you want to shift your life, remove road blocks, or just get happy. So next time you find your feet planted in the kitchen looking for a snack, remember that a bite-size opportunity for personal transformation is waiting to be served up.

Like spices, a little introspection goes along way.

May every meal time be super soul healing time.

Keep on cooking in the kitchen. Together we transform.

Rachael J. Avery, CFSP hosts monthly intuitive cooking classes and workshops for adults, sings with kids during their cooking class, and is a Certified Food & Spirit Practitioner using Chakra Food Healing to help healers balance their inner yumminess. She is the mother of children's book character Netty Noo whom finds friends in nature and author of the *30 Day Social Media Detox*. She lives in Tampa, FL recovering from a 15 year corporate robot career by being human, bobbing in the pool, snacking on organic gluten free sweet potato burgers at noon on Tuesday, and flirting with nature. Visit www.thegratefulpantry.com.

Emotional Healing as a Path to Higher Consciousness

By Juliet Mathison

As the Great Cycle completed itself in 2012, it became apparent that the Shift of the Ages has indeed become a global concept, embraced across all corners of our beautiful planet in myriad ways. We live in a time of unprecedented opportunity for personal and planetary transformation. We see the fear-based, old-order paradigms crumbling all around us, unable to sustain themselves in the presence of the new consciousness that we are birthing as we choose to live our lives on purpose. Living on purpose means that we are able to grasp the essence of our experience within the context of what is happening in the collective consciousness of humanity as it awakens. It means that we know that we have what it takes to be deliberate creators through the act of congruent choice making. It is here that a deeper understanding of the emotional body becomes necessary.

The emotional body is often misunderstood. Let us examine it together for a moment. Emotion represents the water element, it is fluid and changing. It is like the weather, a coherent system of energetic variances that constantly moves to restore balance and flow. It is the *nature* of the emotional body to express. Express means to press out. This is how it moves, by pressing out. Suppression or denial of this natural process creates a distortion that imprints the entire holographic human matrix with a disharmonious frequency that is constantly seeking release. This, of course, translates into biochemical representations of imbalance, which in turn impacts many other levels of our experience. Frequency precedes chemistry.

Humanity has been living in the collective field of fear-based, old-order paradigms for eons of time. These societally imposed codes of behavior and their corresponding belief systems have kept the emotional body in a chronic state of denial and suppression. This distorted state of contracted density manifests both collectively, as a deeply dysfunctional society, and personally, as our own inner turmoil. The internal manifestation presents itself in several ways. We sometimes feel overwhelmed by our emotions because, when something triggers us, it is accessing a storehouse of similar energy that was never allowed to be released at an earlier time. It is rather like a pressure cooker, about to blow the lid off itself. We may judge ourselves (or a loved one may do that for us), as being irrational and overreacting and so we shut down or dissociate. Some of us perform a kind of spiritual bypass surgery on ourselves, literally "spiritualizing the emotion to death" in an attempt to avoid feeling something that has been deemed "negative."

These avoidance mechanisms are born from judgments and false beliefs about our emotional nature. All such approaches are counterproductive, since they deny the fact that it is *the nature* of the emotional body to express, to *press out*. All body systems, both subtle and dense, move constantly; they can do no other. Life is movement and movement is change. The emotional body moves by means of expression. It needs to be *allowed to be what it is*. This is where true healing begins.

Weather the Storm

Let's look at the nature of emotion from a different perspective. Have you ever been out on the beach or up on the mountain when a huge thunderstorm came up out of nowhere and caught you full on? As you reflect on that experience, what do you notice? Do you see that you were feeling all the power and energy of the storm as it moved through, yet at the same time you were the *observer* of that storm, you did not lose your identity to it, nor did you try to resist it? This is how your emotional body is designed to function. It is the weather of your daily experience. Let it be. Show up for it fully. Be as present as you can when the storm comes. Understand that in many cases it will carry the charge of past suppression seeking release. Know that this is an opportunity for you to clear old density that has held you back from the natural flow of your own expansion.

The practice of being fully present for your emotion will allow you to access the deep well of inner peace that lies *underneath* it. It is essential to relinquish any impulse to engage the mind in the storyline of whatever triggered the emotion. Just breathe with the feeling as it arises. The way to move through it is to let it move through you. Something very powerful happens here. We get to receive the gift, the higher purpose of the experience.

It is the nature of consciousness to expand. The contracted

density of denied emotional energy functions as a negative anchor that inhibits the natural momentum of expanding consciousness. When we let the emotional pressure cooker decompress and stay present as the storm passes, we can then unleash the natural tide of expanding consciousness so it can flood in and transform us. It is here that we can *qualify* the energy of that consciousness into the *desired* state in a way that restores peace and balance.

The way to do this is to look for the polar opposite of the emotion being expressed and to activate that quality as an "I am" statement. For example, let's say the emotion I am expressing is "I feel rejected." Once the storm of that feeling has passed, I can now affirm "I am self-appreciating." If you try this method for yourself you will find that it holds a tremendous amount of power. Notice that since an emotion is transient, you say "I *feel* rejected," whereas, the desired state is an aspect of your eternal indestructible consciousness, so it is spoken with permanence, thus "I *am* self-appreciating." The expansive consciousness that floods in has now been qualified to vibrate the specific frequency that directly addresses the pain of the denied emotion. In this way, the inner split is healed. The cosmic organic flow of life is restored and alignment with higher purpose opens up the inner realms for deeper self-awareness.

Once the nature of the emotional body is understood and demystified, we can learn to make friends with the process of healing it. Emotional healing and awakening consciousness are two sides of the same coin. One cannot exist without the other. I have come to love this process, as I know it is a highly effective path to liberation and transcendence. I encourage you to explore the possibilities of this path for yourself. Since you are loved beyond your capacity to understand, you are most definitely, absolutely, worth it.

Juliet Mathison has more than twenty five years of experience in holistic healing and human development. Her passion is to share with others the joyful process of Inner Alchemy; the transmutation of the base metal of suffering into the gold of awakening consciousness. She is a gifted teacher and a pioneer in the field of bio-energetic and psycho-emotional healing. Juliet developed and teaches the Integrative Kinesiology Training Program, an 18 month course of study in accelerated psycho-emotional healing and fifth dimensional energetics. She works with groups, individually by phone or skype, or in person at her office in Sarasota, FL. Visit www.LifeSpectrumInstitute.com.

Love Yourself Just as You Are

By Ivanska Laureano-Tate

My intention for writing this story is to reach as many people as possible to emphasize the importance of self love. Being a massage therapist for more than eight years, I have come to a clear understanding that people just want to feel good, needed, and loved. But somewhere along the way, we forget our initial purpose for being here on earth, as human beings, which is to love ourselves just as we are. We are not to have expectations, which can cause us to feel disappointed and frustrated.

My own journey and experience in losing 100 pounds of excess weight has led me to the realization that the only thing that matters, ultimately, is our relationship with God, Divine Source, Creator or Higher Power.

Putting your trust in this energy — and allowing it to guide and help you create the best experiences possible, those that you are *supposed* to have as a human being — is the most important choice you can make in creating the best possible life here on earth.

Knowing that it does not really matter what others think about you, or even how they might perceive you to be, will set you free. It is what you think about yourself that matters most. So let's put aside the opinions of others and accept that the process of change is the only way to reach a desired goal. Whether it be weight loss issues, kicking bad habits, or dealing with attachments that no longer serve you, nothing is impossible when the desire to change is your primary focus.

Changing old belief patterns about who you are suppose to be or the way you should look or act is an essential part of the journey towards happiness. First, by setting a goal and keeping in mind what you want to accomplish, you set the foundation for your success. Second, you need a detailed plan and the discipline to carry it out. For example, my own experience taught me that I needed to accept the time necessary to create the best possible health for myself through a weight loss plan. I also needed to find a calm moment in my day to connect with God and break away from distractions to achieve the inner peace that was crucial for my transformation.

We all have the ability to feel good and be in balance if we seize the opportunity and choose a direction that will point us toward what we desire to create in life. It is my honor to reveal how simple life can be once we let go of other people's expectations, which can keep us imprisoned.

Winning my battle with dieting and exhaustion has given me the strength to move forward and continue to make the necessary changes that ultimately allowed me to love myself once again. We are all created perfectly well, beautiful and loving, but over the years we tend to lose that connection to our Source, God, and our true nature, which is always perfect. No matter how we were born, within us is a light, a God energy that initially shinned bright. But then others began to put out that light with their opinions and beliefs. Now is the time to ignite that flame once again!

I am a true example of creating an amazing change within my physical being by using the power of the mind in connection to my Divine Source. Along the way, I also learned the benefits of manipulating my energy with Emotional Freedom Technique (EFT), a modality that uses tapping on body meridians to change beliefs. Let my story give you the strength and wisdom to create a great physical state that will allow you to share your much-needed services and joyful moments with those you so dearly care about and the world at large. This is what the Creator intended for us to experience...Love! I leave you with a poem I wrote soon after I reached a level within my being that expresses my reality in words.

I Am That I Am...IVANSKA

WHEN I LOOK BACK IN TIME, I SEE SOMEONE ELSE.
NOT WHO I AM TODAY...

I AM NOW, SOMEWHAT ASCENDED, HIGHER,
ENLIGHTEND...
I AM ALWAYS LEAVING A TRAIL OF LIGHT
WHEREVER I GO, I SHINE SO BRIGHT...

OH I AM STILL HUMAN, I STILL HAVE

PHYSICAL NEEDS HOWEVER, I CAN

FACE FEAR HEAD ON AND THAT FEAR DRIFTS AWAY.

IF I AM TO WALK INTO THE DARK PLACES OF THE SOUL ONCE AGAIN,

I AM QUICK TO REROUTE MY SPIRITUAL NAVIGATION SYSTEM

AND CONTINUE ON MY PATH CONFIDENTLY.

I CARRY WITHIN MY BEING A SENSE OF CALMNESS

AND I FIND SOLACE IN MY TOGETHERNESS WITH GOD.

IN DIFFICULT MOMENTS I AM SLOW TO ANGER

AND QUICK TO RECEIVE WISDOM.

OH HOW GREAT IS THIS KINGDOM...

I WON'T JUDGE

AND OTHERS ENJOY MY COMPANY,

FOR IT IS I THAT HAVE COME TO BRING OTHERS HOPE ON OUR JOURNEY

BACK HOME, WHERE THE DIVINE SOURCE AWAITS

THIS NEW FOUND LOVE....

Ivanska Laureano-Tate is a former licensed massage therapist, healing Reiki Master and a poet at heart who has overcome issues concerning self-love and its effect on weight loss. Her step-father James L. Tate, a self-published author, has been an inspiration for her to write about losing over 100 pounds of excess weight. She found freedom from dieting and fatigue by connecting with her inner-being, re-directing old thought patterns, and using Emotional Freedom Technique. Ivanska reflects on how we can find our true selves and reach our weight loss goals so that we can find that joy and love we origionally came to share with others on this journey we call life.

Take It Off the Mat:
Yoga Philosophies in Life and Business

By Gary Loper

Are you feeling more and more stress lately?

It seems that you cannot go anywhere without people talking about their stresses, or telling you how stressful "these times" are. It is as if we are becoming programmed to believe that life is stressful.

What if there was a way to alleviate the on-going stress, would you be interested?

First, let's take a look at our outside world. Our daily events are coupled with financial pressures, relationship tensions, job changes, various relocations, and chronic illness, what appears to be an overbearing escalation of negative thoughts, emotions, and feelings. It is no wonder many of us are stressed to the max.

One of the first steps is to embrace a healthy way of viewing these challenges—one of acceptance, opportunities for growth, change, and freedom. History has shown repeatedly that change and innovation *only* happens in the midst of chaos and dark times. Is it dark enough for you yet?

How do we migrate through these adversities? How do we discover the positive lessons of these occurrences? There are specific ways of dealing with stress. Rather than resorting to negative internalization and counterproductive responses and actions, such as binge eating, drugs, alcohol, excessive television, or working exorbitant overtime, there is a way to manage the stress. It does not come in a bottle or a pill, and it is not pitched on an infomercial, but has been available for thousands of years and has been shared with us through nature.

The answer is yoga. Customizable to fit into your lifestyle, yoga is the best solution I have found to alleviate on-going stress.

I have been practicing yoga since 1996 and have benefited in many ways—calmness, breath control, strength, connection of the body and mind, a moving meditation, body awareness, and toning. When I have slipped away from my daily practice, I feel my moods shift to places I would prefer they did not go.

At the beginning of 2010, I resolved to practice yoga daily and can very proudly say that I have practiced every day. The biggest benefit has been in stress relief.

In building a new business and taming gremlins, I was feeling very stressed. I truly believe that my yoga practice has helped me keep a reign on my emotions and restored calmness in our home.

The most important aspect of yoga is breathing, keeping control of your breath while your body is in a difficult position. When we notice the breath has become short or nonexistent, we honor the body and move to a place where we maintain breath control and still push the body.

Taking that philosophy off the mat and applying it to our everyday life has incredible benefits. When we get upset, we tend to hold our breath and, while still talking or perhaps yelling, we cut off the air supply to all of our organs and blood. Breath is one of the essential fuels for our bodies to function. Without breath, it is like driving on two flat tires. The vehicle may be drivable for a while, but at what cost?

Starting your own yoga practice is very simple and cost effective. The equipment needed is minimal, and yoga can be practiced anywhere. Although there are a number of incredible videos to practice on your own, I would strongly suggest finding a gifted yoga instructor and taking classes with that individual. The energy of the group class is wonderful, and your instructor will assist you in understanding what you are doing in the best way, to benefit you and your intention.

There are no perfect poses in yoga. Your teacher will show you the direction to go, and it is up to you to honor your body and ignore your ego. Accept the limits of your body. We are all different and have unique experiences that have led us to where we are now. Trying to do what another is doing while your body is telling you "no" will not help, but probably will hurt. You will feel great and alive, and wanting to come back for more, and perhaps in time your body will feel the need to be adjusted all of the time.

Yoga has been derived from observing nature. Watch the animals in or around your home. They are stretching themselves many times a day. How often are you following their lead?

For over 5,000 years, yoga has been the best way to bridge the gap between the body, mind, spirit, and emotions to create balance and embrace acceptance. Yoga can assist you to achieve this acceptance through an overall sense of well-being.

Yoga is more than what it appears to be. Some view it in simplicity, seeing it as another form of exercise. Yoga is far-reaching, the incorporation of breath work, expansion and retraction of the lungs, stretching, and elongating the muscles; it nourishes your entire being. The yoga techniques of breath work and meditation alleviate stress, allowing one to feel a sense of wholeness, well-being, and centering within the experience — one of acceptance no matter where you are in your life. Yoga teaches you to control your mind and body, and restrain the conscious state.

The benefits are immense. It is proven that yoga decreases stress, increases your stamina, improves muscle tone, impedes the aging process, and elevates a creative energy flow. Yoga is enlivening to your entire being! It is a way of life. So, when are you going to get started?

Gary Loper is a recognized Twitter Expert, Mindset/Life/Business Coach, Motivational Speaker/Trainer, former Talk Radio host, respected entrepreneur, Helping People Master the Business of Life. He teaches strategies on how to become successful, to produce and maintain positive solutions, stay in a positive mindset, attract and manifest true wealth. Connect with Gary on Twitter @GaryLoper.

A Path Less Traveled:
Alternative Health Treatments

By Angelica Love Valentine

In the *Ten Rules for Being Human* by Cherie Carter-Scott, the first rule says, "You will receive a body. You may like it or hate it, but it's yours to keep for the entire period." Fortunately for most of us, we are gifted a beautiful body that works perfectly. It may not look or function exactly as we hoped, but from the day we are born, we are blessed with very efficient and effective bodily equipment to get us around in this world.

Early in life, we learn that it's important to keep it running well (good diet, exercise, enough rest, water, etc.). If things start "breaking," we go to a doctor and explain the symptoms so he can identify the source/cause of our problem. The doctor either tells us how to fix it or fixes it for us. But if the doctor can't figure out the cause or doesn't know how to fix the problem, he gives us pills to compensate, and unfortunately we have to put up with side effects, mediocre results, increasing dependence on the pills, premature death, pain, discomfort, misery, etc.

We Have Other Choices

The good news is we also continue to hear and read more and more about alternative/supplemental healing methods taking hold all over the world. And, the resulting testimonials that we hear and read about are all saying the same things—that these healers are able to identify and cure diseases at the source, including diseases that up until recently were labeled as "incurable" by Western medicine. Interestingly, as you start to learn about these alternative treatments, you will begin to see that most of these methods focus on more than the physical aspects and location of disease.

Please note that the healing methods below are only examples of alternative healing modalities. There are many, many, many more that are not listed here; and according to www.wikipedia.com, there are hundreds. The ones used in this article are selected primarily because they are widely recognized.

<u>Acupuncture</u> "is a collection of procedures involving penetration of the skin with needles to stimulate certain points on the body. In its classical form it is a characteristic component of traditional Chinese medicine (TCM),

a form of alternative medicine, and one of the oldest healing practices in the world. According to traditional Chinese medicine, stimulating specific acupuncture points corrects IMBALANCES in the flow of qi (chi) through channels known as meridians." (Source: Wikipedia)

Johrei "(literally "purification of the spirit"), sometimes spelled "Jyorei," is a healing ritual that claims to use "divine light" to dissolve the SPIRITUAL IMPURITIES that are the source of all physical, emotional, and personal problems. It was by developed in Japan in the 1930s by Mokichi Okada. The purpose of channeling universal energy is to cleanse one's spiritual body of the 'clouds' or toxins accumulated over time. In essence, receiving Johrei is like taking a spiritual bath. Johrei claims to raise the spiritual vibration of the person receiving it, resulting in mental, physical, and emotional balance." (Source: www.wikipedia.com)

Pranic healing (created/rediscovered by Grandmaster Choa Kok Sui) uses prana (energy) to heal ailments in the body by manipulation of the person's ENERGY FIELD. Pranic healing is like acupuncture and yoga in that it treats the "energy body," which in turn affects the "physical body." According to Choa Kok Sui, in ancient China there were five levels of healing. The first being massage...The third uses acupuncture...The fifth level, which required the highest level of skill, was the projection of chi without the use of physical contact or needles. The projection of chi energy (pranic energy) without physical contact is called Medical Chi Kung in China. (Source: Wikipedia and www.riverdalewellnesscenter.com)

Reconnective Healing "uses the light and information exchange of the fifth-dimensional energy grid to renew the human body, mind, and spirit. Thus, the effects of a healing session may be felt on the physical, mental, emotional, and spiritual levels. Recognizing that 'healing' means RECONNECTING with the perfection of the universe, we realize that the universe knows what we need to receive." (Source: www.meridianpsych.com)

Reiki "is a spiritual practice developed in 1922 by Japanese Buddhist Mikao Usui. It uses a technique commonly called palm healing or hands-on healing as a form of alternative medicine and is...classified as oriental medicine by some professional medical bodies. Through the use of this technique, practitioners...are transferring UNIVERSAL ENERGY (i.e., reiki) in the form of qi (Japanese: ki) through the palms, which...allows for self-healing and a state of equilibrium." (Source: www.wikipedia.com)

Shamanism "The functions of a shaman may include either guiding...the souls of the dead...and/or curing (healing) of ailments. The ailments may be either purely physical afflictions (such as disease, which may be cured by gifting, flattering, threatening, or wrestling the disease-spirit)…or…mental (including psychosomatic) afflictions…which may be likewise cured by similar methods." (Source: www.wikipedia.com)

Tesla Metamorphosis "has the intent to bring the frequency of light in the human body into perfect balance. Any illness, being manifested physically, mentally, or emotionally, is a result of an IMBALANCE of the universal life-force within the body, which is visible as a frequency of light. Once the balance of the frequency of LIGHT is reestablished, the healing takes place, on all levels." (Source: www.teslametamorphosis.com)

Theta Healing "Theta Healing is essentially applied quantum physics. Using a theta brainwave, which until now was believed to be accessible only in deep sleep or yogi-level meditation, the practitioner is able to connect with the energy of Universal Divine Energy of the Creator of All That Is, to identify issues with and witness healings on the physical body, and to identify and change limiting beliefs. Theta Healing is an extraordinary new technique that allows for immediate physical and emotional transformations and healings." (Source: www. dnathetahealing.com)

What Can I Do Now?

Be THANKFUL because I have so many choices on where to go to get help if I don't feel good. Be GRATEFUL for my body every day, and be grateful for every little thing that IS working in it. Do the things I BELIEVE are "right" or "good" habits to be healthy. Learn to be in touch with my body. LISTEN to it, talk with it, take time to get present to any aches/pains/issues every day and be proactive to figure out what's going on and what to do about it. Go to a doctor if I have a problem or concern; but, if the doctor can't help me fix the problem—BEFORE I start taking a pill—look into alternative healing methods first and find someone who can FIX the problem at the SOURCE.

Angelica Love Valentine is a certified business & life coach helping her clients produce fast, lasting results in business and in life by applying cutting edge technologies for change. With over 15 years of experience and 13 certifications, Angelica Love offers 13 different areas of expertise: Transformation, Manifestation, Business, Money, Life, Communication, Relationships, Belief Work, Spirituality, Health, Consciousness/ Enlightenment, and Executive Skills/ Leadership. Angelica Love is also an experienced coaches' coach. Send her an email at love(at) angelicalovevalentine.com or check out her website to learn more www.angelicalovevalentine.com.

SECTION V:
LIVING WITH PURPOSE

A Christmas Promise: to Live Vibrantly

By Kathy "Katica" Rivera Wallace

It is with great honor that I share with you a glimpse of my transformation story. This transformation was so profound it changed the course of my professional and personal life, culminating in the realization of my new lifestyle brand, Katica: Living Vibrantly (www.katicatv.com).

It was Christmas 2011 and my husband and I were simply grateful we had survived another financially and emotionally challenging year. After being on top of our market, our family business was hit hard in the 2008 economic downturn. Before the collapse, my husband, David, and I grew the family business to three offices and fifty-six employees. By the end of 2011, we were barely holding on with one office and only eight employees. I can never fully express in words the emotional state we endured as we realized we had to lay off team members due to circumstances beyond our control. It was heart wrenching.

I remember that day so vividly. It was the day before Christmas that I finally honored my feelings and gave it a voice. I shared with David that I wanted something for Christmas; he looked perplexed. We had opted earlier that season to do what we had done for the past two Christmases; no gift exchange between the two of us. We had a very limited budget.

I still remember David's confused expression as I started talking. It did not deter me though. "I feel life is meant to be lived differently, David. And we need to figure this out. We don't sleep well, we are not happy, we have both gained a tremendous amount of weight, we are living under chronic stress, we don't exercise, and we don't eat healthy. So, I have an idea." I continued, "Let's commit to each other to take control of what we can control…us. I propose we make a commitment on Christmas Day to eat healthier, manage our weight, and incorporate exercise in our daily life. Let's agree to start in February."

Within four months of eating healthier and incorporating exercise like walking and biking, I had lost a significant amount of weight.

The kicker was when we attended a funeral for a client's wife in June, 2012. We had not seen each other since before Christmas, and he immediately thought David had remarried. He was so stunned with my overall physical transformation that he told me later on that I had inspired him to get healthier and exercise, as well.

After that funeral, a light bulb went off. I was happy with the physical transformation, but I wanted more. My soul yearned for more. There was a mind and spiritual aspect of my being that I felt was being ignored, one that needed nurturing probably even more than the physical aspect of my life.

"Ask it shall be given to you." Matthew 7:7

Four months later, in October 2012, life presented me with an opportunity to go to Mexico, joining a friend to teach at children's homes and orphanages. Even though I did not know how we were going to pay for the trip, I felt blessed with the opportunity. God is great, and somehow the money worked out and off I went on this amazing trip to work with children.

What I experienced in Mexico was nothing short of a rebirth. I thought my purpose on the trip was to teach the children English, when in reality the kids were teaching me on so many levels. They taught me about life, about each other, relationships, reality, etc. I saw the face of happiness in places that I would have never imagined it to be. I saw love expressed in ways that inspired me. These kids changed my life forever. I read books, prayed, met people, exercised, and spent all my free time in nature, usually by the water, all of which inspired me to continue on my journey.

I remember praying to God asking Him many times, "What is the real reason I came to Mexico?" His answer was simple: *Allow the authentic self to emerge permanently and your life will change forever.* There was so much more for me to learn...

When I returned from Mexico later that month, life was not easy. I felt as if I my energy had shifted; yet my routine in the United States was the same. So I decided to continue to live as I had in Mexico: I changed my eating habits, the time I ate, the way I lived, what I did, I even limited TV. I loved having an existence without all the noise we have here in our lives. When I brought my new routine home, it felt right and comfortable. I did not feel out of sync and unhappy. I continued to immerse myself in research of the body, mind, and spirit to expand knowledge. By Christmas

2012, I felt empowered and excited as I continued on my journey.

On January 2013, I attend my first hypnosis/hypnotherapy workshop, and I was hooked. By end of May 2013, I was certified in Hypnotherapy, Qigong (a traditional Chinese breath and movement exercise working with energy, Chi), and a Food Healing program. Between February 2012 and July 2013 I had lost 34 pounds, and I had never felt better. My hair, skin, nails and other outward signs of health were all notably improved. Most compelling were the internal changes: unlimited energy, a positive outlook, and a general sense of well-being were reflecting a lifestyle that was conducive to a vibrant life. I wanted to share this life-changing knowledge and process with others, though I somehow knew that I wanted to do it on a bigger scale. The answer was yet another step in my transformation.

This was the direction I was to take to teach others on a broader scale how to live vibrantly. The result is Katica: Living Vibrantly, a lifestyle brand that brings all of these ideas to life, in a format that scales from one-on-one interaction to global distribution. On October 1st, we launched our very first live broadcast from Tampa, FL, in English and Spanish. The basic premise of the show is that life starts to become more vibrant once we align body, mind, and spirit. I know because I am walking proof.

Final affirmation came in March 2014, just four months after we aired our first live show; we were nominated in four categories for the 2014 Tampa Bay Talkie Awards: Best Female Host, Best Lifestyle Show, Best Empowerment Show, and Best International Show. This was the final confirmation that I was aligned with my purpose, something that happened because I took those first small steps down the path that ultimately transformed my life. A Christmas Promise: to Live Vibrantly.

Kathy "Katica" Rivera Wallace lives her own brand, Living Vibrantly. Katica earned her degree in business and marketing. After years of the corporate grind, Katica worked with her husband to grow their family business, as she continued volunteering in her community. Her naturally giving spirit was reinvigorated through these experiences, leading her on a path of self-improvement with an emphasis on gaining knowledge and certifications that would allow her to help others Live Vibrantly. She achieved certifications in Hypnotherapy, Qi Gong and Food Healing. Through her award-winning webcast, *Katica: Living Vibrantly*, that seeks to help her audience live a vibrant life by aligning body, mind and spirit. Visit www.katicatv.com.

Awakening My True Self and Releasing the Victim

By Rebecca Edwards

Awakening to my soul's purpose was a gift I received from excavating my true Self from the dark depths of self-defeating behaviors, victimhood, and addiction. Aligning with the powerful energy of this process allowed me to see, with new eyes, how my greatest afflictions became my greatest assets. The courage I found in my life by becoming the person I was meant to be changed the pain of the past. As I awakened to my truth, I was granted the opportunity to transform my pain by inspiring change in those who still suffer. And as I fell into alignment with both love and service, I began to share my transformational story to help others grow spiritually.

My Experience

I was an actress, and the stage was my life. It became the setting for my drama. My script consisted of all the wrongs, misfortunes, and injustices I had personified. My elaborate stories of woe defined me, ruled my thoughts and my actions, and habitually fed my fears of never having enough or ever getting what I wanted. The more I spoke of suffering, the more momentum suffering received. The more loudly resentments echoed, the more toxic my view of life became. I was, unknowingly, feeding a psychic parasite that grew stronger with every judgment against what life offered me. I desperately wanted to be free of this spiritual sickness, but it was everyone else who had to change so I could be happy. My personal power was diminished by negative patterns of chronic complaining and constant blaming of others for my unhappiness. As long as I was a victim of others "bad behavior" I was trapped by the story I was telling myself.

Eventually my story lost its appeal; I turned to alcohol to "alter my distorted perception of reality." I lost my place in the script, and I could no longer play my part. I sank into the abyss of emotional nothingness, defeated by alcohol, resentments, and a painful childhood. My story claimed victory.

The Awakening

As I lay crushed under a pile of lost dreams, broken promises, and self-pity, my tears of desperation gave vital water to deeply planted seeds of hope. In brokenness, I found the courage to surrender the attachment to my story. In the darkest moment of my life, a warm light surrounded me. In that light, I connected with a power greater than myself. That day my story became the catalyst for change. I was finally at the point where I was willing to receive help from a counselor and a 12 Step program. Rewriting the story of my life was no longer a future event; it was the reality of today if I committed to do the work required.

Acceptance-Ending Denial

With change came a great deal or personal responsibility. I had to embrace the past, tell the truth, identify with my pain and loss, and purge my darkest secrets of what I experienced as a child: sexual abuse, emotional abandonment, and complete chaos. I had to be willing to sit with the emotional pain of mourning an interrupted childhood. I had to learn to be still and accept each feeling that was bubbling to the surface. By taking the time to heal slowly and thoroughly, I learned how I could utilize a variety of resources that were instrumental in helping me change. Each transformational step I took aided in the quieting of my mind. This endless mental chatter was always related to fear. When I became still, the person I was pretending to be and the vision of who I wanted to become formed the bridge that connected the two worlds I was trapped between.

Forgiving Myself and Others

With help from those resources, including the 12 Step program, a trauma/addiction counselor, and several highly recommended transformational books, I was shown how to forgive myself and those who, through their spiritual sickness, injured me or caused pain. As a result, I was set free from the barbed chains of anger, resentment, and hopelessness. Releasing toxic emotions set my soul free. Once I could look at each experience for the gift rather than the curse, my mind began to focus on joy rather than sorrows. I began to see how my experience could help others be set free from victimization and catastrophizing. Healing through forgiveness changed my past by allowing me to look at it differently. I can now reach into the lives of others and deeply touch their hearts. By sharing my story, others can embark on their own transformation from pain and lack to healing and abundance.

Loving Unconditionally

Unconditional love of self and others was the spiritual key that unlocked a new vision for a purposeful life. The enlightened state of consciousness that I was identifying with brought more depth to my life, my relationships, my work, and how I viewed those in my circle of friends and those within my community. A richer, more serene life was the result of *letting go* of what no longer served my higher purpose.

> *Today, I have a choice of how I think, how I communicate, and how I spend precious time that creates each new moment of life. I am either in love or fear. Neither exists in each other.*

I began to resonate with the reflection of whom I was becoming. I was able to gently flow with the cycles of life instead of going against them. I could be still with gratitude instead of being restless with judgments that were fueled by self-centered thoughts. I soon craved the guidance of those who came before me in the evolution of the spirit. *"Letting go"* continued to be the key of emotional freedom when fears of loss, lack, scarcity or injury resurfaced. I learned regardless of circumstances, life is meant to be lived with ease and joy. When I saw life as an experienced teacher, I was less afraid of everything that did not fit within my understanding of what life was supposed to be. Loving my path and my story excavated the truth of my soul's purpose.

Rebecca Edwards is an inspirational author thriving in a Universe that yields to her desires to be a catalyst for spiritual change. Her own journey of transformation through life's most difficult circumstances has awakened within her a deep passion to share her personal story. The words of Paramahansa Yogananda echo her soul's true purpose, "As the sun spreads vital rays of light, I will spread rays of hope in the hearts of the poor and forsaken, and kindle a new strength in the hearts of those who think they are failures". Visit RebeccaLEdwards. com or Rebecca@RebeccaLEdwards.com.

Dance in Your Own Shoes and Follow Your Passion

By Arielle Giordano

Dance like there is nobody watching as you dream with your feet!

Following our heart leads us to our passion and truest desires in both career and personal relationships. When we question, "Is this right for me?" or "Is this true for me?" and then listen quietly to our deepest knowing, we hear the answer from our voice of true understanding and choice. It moves with the insight to *know*, the courage to move forward, and the confidence to take action and trust in the process. I write this to awaken us to listen to what we know in our heart, follow our passion, and dance like there is nobody watching!

Not long ago, I resigned from my position as chairperson for an international university. This was a huge step for me to take both personally and professionally. For many years, my fears, patterns, emotions, thoughts, beliefs, perceptions, self criticisms, judgments, shame, and survival issues surfaced when I needed to make choices. When offered this job, I knew it did not feel right, but I listened to the voice of my survival issues and signed the contract anyway. Although, the "free spirit" inside of me said to let the job go and move forward, my own insecurity, conditioning, and "old" ways of being motivated me to accept the position.

Prior to letting the job go, I was drawn to a woman at a networking event. We connected immediately, as if we already knew each other! I hired her as my life coach, and at our first meeting I shared my thoughts and feelings regarding my position. I was squeezing myself into a tiny "job box," like a genie in a bottle, consumed by trying to fit in for minimal financial rewards. There was little passion, energy, or opportunity to express my true Self. Her answer was, "Quit your job!"

A big red flag went up inside me: "I can't quit my job!" I can't lose integrity and breach my contract, I told her. She said, "If you are not being true to yourself, then you are out of integrity with yourself." I knew what she was saying was true; it tingled in my body, and the body knows before the mind.

I recognized that my creative flow was blocked by this job. I was not connecting to my inner flow and dancing my own dance. I realized I was dancing in someone else's shoes and doing someone else's job! Where was my self-worth and value? During the coaching, I participated in an abandonment recovery program, and it helped me realize that I had abandoned myself!

I knew it was time for me to quit the job. After sending the resignation email, I felt mentally and emotionally drained and physically ill. However, during this process I learned to dance with my fears rather than block them and let them hold me back.

Just after sending the email there was a knock at the door. It was the lawn man, handing me a tiny white rubber dog that he found. Immediately, I was reminded of my Native American animal medicine cards; the Dog is a symbol for loyalty with the question, "Are you being true to yourself and your goals?" The following day, I connected with an empowerment center and was asked by one of the owners to teach dance and facilitate expressive arts and transformational workshops.

When I told her I quit my job, she said that astrologically I was at a time of profound and great changes. The same day, I completed writing an *Abnormal Psychology* textbook project, and I was invited to coauthor, *Transform your Life*. Later at the post office, I ran into the owner of a local bookstore and discussed the possibility of a book signing. Serendipity?

Learning Lessons

From this experience, I learned that my choices and decisions were based upon fears, inherited patterns, values, beliefs, and social conditions. I was living in a continuous state of anxiety, operating in survival mode, with adrenaline on high volume. I was afraid to live and "just be." I was like a doll, tightly wound and bound, afraid to unravel and be true to my career passions and allow loving relationships in my life. Real desires, talents, and abilities were buried underneath my tender but painful childhood experiences.

As soon as my survival patterns came up, I danced the sidestep into a more traditional job rather than dancing with my passions. At the same time, these deep-rooted patterns were hurting my love relationship. So, in addition to changing my career path, I gradually opened my heart to my fiancé and let love happen—and now we are learning to dance together on many new levels. The healing of my past is about me reconnecting, rediscovering, and uncovering parts of me that I had forgotten.

What matters the most to me is dancing down to the bare bones, into the soles and rawness of my feet! I have released old patterns, feelings, and emotions, and bought new awareness to light. I am now living life dancing to the rhythm of my own heart, being present and in my body, and in the flow!

Awareness brings light to the surface, so let your heart dance
in the light and express your true Self.

My advice to you: Dance like there is no one watching in a loving gentle space with openness and softness, without judgment, criticism, or ridicule. Dance with your passion, courage, fearlessness, confidence, and trust to gracefully become a new you!

Here are some ways to make powerful choices and to discover and follow your passions:

- Follow your passion with courage, confidence, and trust.
- Let the knowing in your heart guide you to your passions, which requires real honesty.
- Discern the repetition of conditioned patterns from the "real you." (Are you dancing in your own shoes or in someone else's?)
- Know that it is okay to become unstuck and move forward.
- Stretch and move out of the old, normal way of being, and let yourself be different.
- Know that goodness moves in many ways and we are never given more than we can handle; enjoy being new and fresh every day.
- When thoughts, feelings, beliefs patterns, perspectives or issues come up, make a conscious, powerful choice to move forward through the fears.

Begin to move in the "awesomeness" of a child; be childlike snf playful, do what you love, and have fun!

Arielle Giordano has a Master's in Counselor Education and a Master's in Educational Leadership and is a faculty member and Lead Faculty Area Chairperson for the College of Humanities, History and the Arts at the University of Phoenix. She is a published author of several books and magazine articles. In 2014, she published an Instructor's Manual for Barlow Abnormal Psychology 4th ed. In 2013, she wrote *Psychology, A Journey 3rd.ed. Study Guide* published by Nelson Education, Toronto, ON. Arielle has been a featured guest on radio and television and other media across the US and Canada. She offers dance classes, dancing for emotional release workshops and creative expression seminars. Visit dancingfromtheinsideout.com.

Letting Go of "How"

By Dana Feldmeier

As I walked the hallway, my stomach was in knots. After teaching public school for 6 years, I was about to change the course of my career path, and life. It didn't seem like that long ago that I entered the same office for the interview that concluded with my first post-college job as a 3rd grade teacher.

My love for teaching remained, but my soul was nudging me to make a change. It started when I saw a video online for nutrition school. Typically a thorough analyzer, I signed up for this education program within a few days of watching the video. Something inside me just knew I needed this.

I graduated and became a certified health coach. Sure, I had "a plan" as to how to go out and begin my new business venture, but saying goodbye to a regular salaried position was scary! I decided to ease my way into this and live at a yoga ashram where I knew I would have a roof over my head and food in my belly in exchange for service as I worked out this "plan."

Yoga came into my life a few years earlier, a gift from god, to help with the stress of teaching and aid in healing a broken heart. Through yoga I learned to meditate: to sit with the thoughts, emotions, fears, and worries; the mental chatter that was part of daily life. I dove in head-first, sensing the power behind this ancient practice and attended a 10-day silent mediation retreat.

I moved into the yoga center after this retreat, where I was able to spend six months immersed in a spiritual community and meditation became a part of my daily life. Growing up catholic, I knew about prayer, but it wasn't until I learned to meditate that I realized I could HEAR God answering my questions and prayers, offering guidance and suggestions. This did NOT happen right away. In fact, at first, my mind seemed to go crazy as I sat in stillness. The thoughts raced at the speed of light. But then in the days and week to follow, as I continued to keep up with the practice, little signs and answers to my questions began to appear. Not during the meditations typically, but some other time of day.

Was this real? There was something out there actually listening in on my thoughts, desires, and prayers? I began to put this theory to the test and asked for signs. "Okay, God, if you are real, I'd like a pink flower today." Imagine my surprise when a woman came up to me and handed me a pink flower the next day. Still, the mind popped in again—just a coincidence? After all, the pink flower arrived one day after I requested it. I asked for more signs. I was patient, and they came. When I lost patience, I prayed for patience and it was returned, along with a sign. For real?

My games and daily chats with God continued as I chopped vegetables, folded laundry, hiked the rocky pathways of the Blue Ridge Mountains, and sat amongst the rocks and trees. I have always loved nature, but this period of my life allowed me to soak up its wisdom in a whole new way. Abundance and beauty were everywhere, and nothing in nature rushed or hurried.

When my mind traveled back to "how" everything was going to work and away from the present moment, the teachings of yoga and nature remind me to relax and let everything unfold. I also began to differentiate between taking action verses taking inspired action, which never feels forced or rushed.

I learned about the power of meditation not only when sitting still, but all day long, while engaged in daily tasks.

I believe we are each guided here with unique gifts and a message to spread. If we are too busy figuring out the "how" ourselves, there is no space for God's magic and gifts. The message I wish to share, or that God is sharing through me, is that you have an internal guidance system and truly you are never alone. Right now you are surrounded by beings of love and contain within you a universal energy force that can never be extinguished. Yes, you came with a battery pack and you are the recharge station! As you allow your soul time to be still and recharge, the "how" of your life will unfold in a magical way beyond what you can imagine.

After dreaming of life near the ocean, I ended up in a beach town that was a perfect fit for me and developed a business that allowed my soul the time freedom it desired. It started as an inkling, followed by a big leap of faith and a pink flower delivered one day late, which was of course, perfect timing.

Dana Feldmeier is a certified health coach and essential oil expert. As a former public school teacher, she witnessed the health crisis and over-use of medication first hand. She is passionate about starting little ones on the path to wellness at an early age and believes the best way to do this is to educate and empower mothers! Through sharing essential oils, remarkable gifts from the earth, as medicine, she empowers women to heal and treat their families naturally! Visit her website: www.SmartCookieNutrition.com to learn more.

Living Life on Purpose

By Coach Dianne Kipp

The most powerful gift of coaching is discovering your own truth. All of us have the ability to Live Life on Purpose, to follow our dreams, so why don't we? We "go to sleep" and run life on autopilot. If we take time to find our "authentic self" we can make conscious choices based on fact to create purposeful lives. We must "look" and "see" the facts to discern when "emotions and stories" are interfering with our ability to *consciously choose* the *best* next step for realizing dreams. Through 10 years of professional experience as an ontological coach, I now help people "wake up" their authentic selves and live lives with purpose.

Falling Asleep – Your Brain Working FOR or AGAINST You?

Picture an iceberg. Scientists at Stanford, MIT, and other esteemed institutions have determined that the human mind operates like an iceberg: the 10 percent that's visible (above the surface) is your **Conscious Mind** and the 90 percent that's hidden (below the surface) is your **Subconscious Mind**.

As infants our subconscious mind is clear, blank. As we grow and experience life, we gather information resulting in beliefs, values, and conclusions. Because our subconscious mind is capable of processing three times that of our conscious mind…the subconscious mind *"drives our bus."*

In essence, our subconscious is a vast collection of unintentional, habitual thoughts and behaviors. No surprise when we are thinking about trying something new, how our mind gives us only the reasons *it won't work.*

Our psyche is leftover from Neanderthal times, when fight, flight, or freeze was our defense against danger. Result: our "subconscious protector" can "scream" us into submission and keep us *stuck in the past.*

Learning to make conscious choices sans emotion lets us "take authentic action" to get what we desire, with confidence, clarity, and ease.

Waking Up

Becoming "conscious" or "waking up" involves spending time **"mindfully."** Getting quiet and focusing your attention on your breath allows your mind to settle and brings awareness of your thoughts.

Ask yourself, "What do I want to leave as my legacy?"

1. **Get clear on what matters most to you**, prioritized into the top three items.
2. **Recognize your "Monkey Mind,"** (fabricated worse-case stories) and discern facts from fiction *before* choosing next steps.
3. **Focus your attention and energy** on getting the top three items done.

Choosing to live life consciously is a *most courageous act*. It enables you to lead and live your life *on purpose*. Determining what matters most and demonstrating your most authentic self is your personal "roadmap" for discovering that purpose. It ignites your passion to "get busy" leaving the legacy you intend.

I'm blessed to *live my life on purpose*: coaching others to discover and live *their* purpose. Here's how you can "coach yourself" to get "unstuck:"

While being "mindful," ask yourself these questions when feeling stuck, overwhelmed, or undecided. The key is to answer while looking inside for the "truth." Be honest with yourself, no one else is listening.

1. What is the absolute worse part of this situation for you?
2. What do you hate or dislike most about it?
3. Keep going by continuing to ask, "What is the worse part?" and "What do I really hate about this?" You will begin to see what lies at the base of your belief.

   Examples: I feel trapped. I don't want the responsibility. I want freedom. Things don't change. It costs too much money. Someone else won't like it (mother, husband, friend).

4. Now, look at what you discovered. Is it based in current fact, or an old idea?
5. Ask, "Is this still true for me?" If '**yes**', is it OK with you? This lets you see your own truth, rather than acting from an old idea. If it is still true and you're OK with it, great! You are conscious, awake, and clear.
6. If there is something you want to change or share with someone, what might that be?
7. Are you willing to make that change or have the conversation to take the next step toward getting what you want? If "**yes**," *commit* to a date when you will do it.
8. Congratulate yourself for moving forward, and ask a friend to check with you on your success. Then celebrate together on getting it done!

How can this be applied to relationships?

Ask yourself these questions, answering either "Yes" or "No." *There is no option for "maybe."* Listen to your heart; the answer is there, I promise.

   A. Is this person "it" for you? Meaning for the "rest of your life."
   B. Is this person's energy supportive of you and your intentions?
   C. *If yes*, great! Isn't it awesome to know you are sure?
   D. *If no*, and you feel it, and you want to make a change, you must let the person know.

Stepping forward with compassion and in full truth allows both of you to decide the next steps. A simple statement, "This is not working for me," prevents blame or feelings of guilt for both of you. You may discover it is what your partner wants as well. Either way, your honesty gives him or her a choice. Not easy, but truly the kindest and most compassionate thing you can do.

Life is Short, Live it Well

Living life purposely is a most satisfying feeling. Just a few examples of how ignoring negative mind chatter moved me from "dreaming to reality:"

- Owned a live-aboard sailing-snorkeling business in Caribbean.
- Founded Follow Your Heart Journeys and Dianne M. Kipp, LLC (the work of my dreams!).
- Led adventure tour/retreat groups for women.
- Rode a 100-mile bike ride at 65 honoring my dad, raising $4,000 for JDRF.

I leave you with an invitation to *live your life on purpose* by choosing "mindfully" to do so. "Being" your authentic self, "doing" what you love, and "having" what you desire *truly* is your choice.

Are you willing? Sure you are, so go ahead and do it! Now
that's being Courageous!

Dianne M. Kipp, BSN, PCC, CTT, Certified Life & Executive Coach, has empowered her clients to conceive and achieve their most important life and professional ambitions for the past 10 years. Author, speaker, and retreat facilitator, she loves to ask, "Would it be OK if life got easier?" Respected as a "transformation architect," she has profoundly shifted the lives of many. Nominated Iconic Woman 2012, Top 3 Women Entrepreneurs, Dianne's own life is a perfect example of "courageously living *life-on-purpose*". She welcomes 'life-purpose seekers', executives, and groups, wanting to move from "good-life to great-life" while making unique contributions for the benefit and well being of all. Visit www.diannekipp.com.

What Does Life Purpose Mean to Me?

By Dolores J. Gozzi

Life Purpose has many meanings and interpretations depending on each individual. When I ask, "What is your Life Purpose?" most people say to have a good job; to be with family; or to be a good citizen. These statements are all great goals, but they are only scratching the surface of Life Purpose. We need to dig deeper because true Life Purpose is using our gifts, talents, and skills to create the life and lifestyle that will fulfill our divine plan for being on earth.

Life Purpose is "unique" for each individual — as it should be. Some will know that their Life Purpose is to reach out to the world and share their gifts, like a Dali Lama. Then there is the individual who knows how to guide her family — and she's the person everyone goes to for support and guidance. She could be a "life coach" not only for her family, but for others as well. While not everyone is destined to be a world-renowned spiritual leader, we still need to recognize that each and every person plays a vital role in and contributes to the world in many wonderful ways!

That said, there are many paths and roads that we travel to find our Life Purpose, and along the way we are faced with different challenges to help us grow. Without growth, we stand idle and do not give ourselves the opportunity to LIVE fully and experience what the world has to offer. We also need to be reminded that we cannot always fall back on the same gifts and talents we were born with. We come to earth to learn, as well as to share, and by facing challenges we grow and learn new skills to weave into our lives over time. Moreover, some of us know at a very young age what those talents and gifts are, but we don't always know how to share them, so this can become another part of the journey.

Once we are aware of our talents and gifts, we have a foundation to build on. As a result, our environment begins to change, and we see shifts in our home, the city or town where we live, and in how our location impacts our life and lifestyle. For example, an individual who is helping others is likely to strive to establish a tranquil and peaceful home, while someone working in the computer industry or programming is likely to invest in designing a high-tech living environment.

Others may have the perfect home for their Life Purpose, but do not have a job that reflects that Life Purpose, and this leaves them frustrated. Those who do begin to incorporate their skills and talents into their current job may get feedback from coworkers that prompts them to branch out into another part-time practice that is more in alignment with their Life Purpose. Some may end up relocating to live in an area that is receptive to their physical body and emotional awareness, while others may utilize the Internet to work from home. The possibilities are as diverse as the people on this planet, and what is right for you will become clear once you come to know *your* unique Life Purpose!

You see, once you begin the process of examining your life to determine your gifts, talents and skills—and ultimately find your Life Purpose—others who complement your world with merge with you and help you to create an environment filled with new possibilities.

If you are wondering how to start on this journey, the following set of questions will help point you in the right direction. Answer without hesitating or thinking too much, and trust your inner guidance.

What does Life Purpose mean to me? (Write down the first thing that comes to your mind.)

What are my talents/skills? (These are the gifts that you were born with, those that come naturally to you.)

Where do I use my talents/skills? (Do you use your gifts 1. at home in your personal life, 2. in your professional life or 3. in both?)

How often do I use my talents/skills as a percentage of my day? (Note the percentage of time during the day you utilize your gifts in 1. your home and personal life and 2. in your professional life.)

Do you value your skills? (Yes or no.)

Do others value your skills (Yes or no.)

What skills do you desire to learn? (Listen to your desires; they usually will give an indication of new skills you should be working on.)

What are my challenges? (These are the lessons you need to learn to move forward in your Life Purpose.)

Do you feel the need to constantly create change? (Yes or no. Constant change can indicate two things. Either you are frustrated in your current life/lifestyle and need to change it often so you can satisfy your soul, or you know that with every change you are achieving the skills you need to move on to the next step. In other words, you are working to get all the pieces of your life into alignment with your Life Purpose.)

Write a summary that outlines where you need to develop in life to find and live your Life Purpose. (Your own thoughts on what feels right for you to do next.)

What does Life Purpose mean to you now? (After finishing this exercise, has it changed? Do you need to look at it from a different angle?)

Answering these questions should give you a clear picture of where you are using your gifts and how you can integrate them into other areas where you are not using them. It also should prompt you to start thinking about the value of your gifts and what you have to offer the world. Be sure to examine the areas you need to work on in both your personal life and professional world. Look at your desires and how you can start to bring them into form and weave them into your current gifts. Look at your challenges as an opportunity to learn. And, most importantly, enjoy the journey!

Dolores J. Gozzi is a speaker, coach, and healer who guides women to follow their heart and lead with their wisdom. She teaches women how to access their gifts, challenges and desires as the core thread of their life purpose. Her nature-inspired programs, oracle readings, women's retreats and creation coaching are designed to educate and empower participants to connect to their unique sacred essence and bring desires naturally into form. Dolores's mission is to support women in reconnecting with their inner strength for transformational change. Dolores offers coaching and healing sessions in nature's classroom where she lives in Florida, via the phone, or online at www.naturescycles.com.

Being "Old":
An Octogenarian's Viewpoint

By Berenice Andrews

It's altogether likely that reaching age 80 could signify an *arrival*... because along with the wrinkles and the other unmistakable signs of being "old," there's the wondrous possibility of being wise.

By the onset of the ninth decade, when the pace of life has slackened a little or a lot, there can be the increasingly welcome opportunities for introspection. Then, while pondering deeply on the meaning and purpose of this lifetime, a person could discover something quite amazing: that during all those years, there has been the steady unfolding of a unique and personal account that's more than just an autobiography and much more than a mere narrative about a lifetime of "doing." There, in the depths awaiting discovery, is a "Sacred Story."

A person's Sacred Story originates in the Spirit, in the time beyond time and, thereafter, continues to grow and develop throughout each lifetime on this Earth plane. Like a deep stream ceaselessly flowing under the autobiography, that Sacred Story carries not only the transcendent energies of one's beingness — life, light, love and law — but also the "dossier" of every past life and all the happenings of this one.

A person's Sacred Story contains the paradoxical truth — *both the causes and the effects* — about one's choices, aware and unaware; about one's relationships, loving and unloving; and about one's beingness, evolved and unevolved.

In sum, a person's Sacred Story reveals not only the meaning of a life but also its immense possibilities...including that of being wise.

In the autobiography from conception to age 80, there can be a few or many detours, dead-ends and drop-outs that are often regarded as "failures," as "wasted efforts," and as "the times of getting nowhere." But, in the Sacred Story they are the necessary preparation for the beginnings that seem to happen accidentally, the breakthroughs that promote new realizations and the encounters that add new dimensions to life.

In the autobiography, there can be the intervals of regret, grief, sometimes despair. Yet, in the Sacred Story those intervals are a "wake-up" call about some of the choices, some of the relationships, some of the periods of being unevolved. Thus, while the life "events" are often regarded as separate parts of the autobiography, they actually coalesce to form the rich substance of the "chapters" in the Sacred Story.

It's a story of becoming: a story that reveals the essential truth about being human on this Earth plane; that without exception, everyone's life has a purpose, that nobody and no-thing are accidents, that people are here by divine appointment and that there's no such thing as a meaningless life.

So, being an octogenarian who has arrived can mean "knowing" this about oneself. It can mean that having lived through a (sometimes) challenging autobiography, it can now be perceived as what it really is: a profound and multidimensional "teaching" a unique and personal lesson indicating one's spiritual evolution...on the paths of getting to be wise. And in that "seeing," one is actually dipping into the underlying Sacred Story and discovering both life's meaning and its awaiting possibilities.

For that "lesson" is an awakened awareness; that even in the darkest moments of the autobiography, there has been an inextinguishable inner Light — a guidance system — that has moved the action forward; an awareness that what has always been necessary has been to focus on and foster an increasingly deep connection with the inner "kingdom" in which that Light dwells. Thus, getting to be wise has also involved realizing the magnitude of one's own beingness, one's own creative humanness. And all of it has actually been the unfolding of a Sacred Story about finding wisdom.

Now, being wise doesn't necessarily mean being erudite and it never means putting on "spiritual" airs. Being wise means having compassionate discernment into the personhood — the unique and sometimes inexplicable parts — of oneself and others. Thus, it often requires the letting go of a reformer's zeal.

Being wise means having compassionate detachment from the world's follies; from taking sides, passing judgments and holding forth about "the good old days." Thus, it often requires the letting be of some (often incomprehensible) situations and circumstances.

Being wise means having compassionate clarity about humanity's somewhat convoluted—but nevertheless, spiritual— evolution and about the spiritual purpose of one's own life. Thus, it often requires patiently allowing the shedding of more light on the subject—humanity and/or oneself.

Above all, being wise means "knowing" that no matter how challenging the autobiography has been (and might continue to be), the Sacred Story will always be about becoming, about culminating into greater beingness. After all, it carries all of life's meaning and possibilities.

Thus, along with the wrinkles and the other unmistakable signs of being "old," an octogenarian can be blessed with a sense of having arrived and with a capacity for savoring every precious moment.

Berenice Andrews is a shamanic teacher/healer and the author of *Rebirthing Into Androgyny: Your Quest For Wholeness, And Afterward.* She writes: "Although my autobiography includes growing up in a mining camp, leaving it, marrying, birthing two children, divorcing, obtaining a 'higher' education and having a professional career, that's just my personal history. My Sacred Story is the one that tells about 'knowing' the indwelling Spirit, losing that awareness, finding it again in an 'awakening,' meeting my shaman teacher, learning the healer's craft, recognizing my life's purpose and thereafter, following my bliss." You may contact Berenice on her web site, thestonecircleclassroom.com.

SECTION VI:
EMBRACING CHANGE

7 Simple Steps to Creating My Intentions

By Rev. Elena C. Jones

There are many lessons learned throughout life. Some people learn best through formal education and training, some by conversation, others in the course of hands-on experience. The way we learn and what we do with the information we are taught is up to us. Living life with purpose, confidence, and trust in Mother/Father God has taught me there are no limits to what can be accomplished. However, I did not embody this lesson without a price to pay. The lessons I learned are shared with you in hopes of blessing your life with limitless peace, joy, love, and prosperity.

"The Seven Simple Steps to Creating My Intentions" is the title of my lessons learned, and I would not have learned these seven steps without going into mediation. During this quiet time I was asked to create a motivational conference. The fact that I received such a request startled me for a moment. In my confusion I heard myself saying, "How can I do this when I only have $79.00 in my checking account?"Spirit confirmed I live in an unlimited universe and everything will be provided for me; all I had to do was trust. Trusting fully by allowing the transformation process of personal and spiritual growth to occur is difficult. From the embryonic stages of development, I have realized this journey of trust, letting go, and fully being in the present moment is what our Creator intended for us all. I want to share with you my journey through these steps:

1. The first thing I had to do was to be clear with my intentions.

2. Second, to make a commitment and stick to it. I knew that to serve up what was being asked of me I needed to first commit to myself as well as the conference.

3. The next step was to write out the intent so I stayed focused. At

the same time, I knew I had to affirm out loud my commitment of my intention. I had not done a conference before and did not know where to turn. Therefore I asked for "the how" from my angels and guides. I had to be open to receive. I wanted all the answers, and they did not come fast enough for me. Since I had not done this before, I knew that I had to ask for help.

4. Asking for help is the fourth step in creating your intentions. I asked for the right people to be shown to me for my highest and the conference's highest good, and they were.

5. Next, the fifth element was revealed to me, which is the plan of action. When plans began coming together, I realized I then needed to let go.

6. In the sixth step of letting go, I realized by getting out of the way Creator/Spirit was able to do the intended work. The real challenge came when I had to sign a contract and provide a deposit I did not have to give. Before I signed the contract and paid the deposit I learned the seventh step.

7. The seventh step is having faith and stepping through the fire to get to the other side. The price I paid was not the monetary value of creating and organizing a motivational conference. The price I paid in this lesson was about letting go and fully trusting. The journey to success in creating my intentions is not about the income or possessions obtained, but about the person each of us can become.

The conference was called "Creating My Intentions," and it took place on Saturday, October 15th, 2011, at the InterContinental Hotel in Tampa, FL. People came from all over. It was magical, and it was divine. As I look back, I am in awe on how incredibly it all unfolded, from the vendors to the speakers. Once I let go, one by one they started showing up. It never ceases to amaze me the power of intention, but it only works when we give ourselves permission to let go and trust in this invisible force that I choose to call God.

I challenge you to become the very best you can, and experience what Mother/Father God will manifest for you. Intention is thinking like God thinks, that nothing is impossible, that all is possible as long as you believe.

Namaste my brothers and my sisters. May the light of our Creator illuminate your path and may you always remember what an incredible co-creator you truly are.

Elena C. Jones has a rich life experience; born in Southern Italy she grew up in Buenos Aires, Argentina, eventually moving to the United States over 40 years ago. She served three years in the United States Air Force. She later studied business and philosophy in academic and authentic environments. Elena has owned and successfully operated Elena C. Jones Productions, a Wedding and Event Company. She was the creator of the first Mind, Body and Spirit, "Creating My Intentions" conference that took place on October 15, 2011 in Tampa, FL. Rev. Elena C. Jones is a self published author of 7 Simple Steps To Creating My Intentions and Connecting The Dots. Visit www.almaquest.net.

The 7 Day Media Cleanse

By Joran Slane Oppelt

"Everyone can perform magic, everyone can reach his goals, if he is able to think, if he is able to wait, if he is able to fast."
— Hermann Hesse, Siddhartha

It wasn't even my idea. It was my seven-year-old daughter, Alchemy, who suggested it. "Daddy, let's go a week without watching TV!"

Her mother, Jennifer, and I had just finished our second juice cleanse of the year, and I think Alchemy was caught up in all the cleansing and fasting and wanted somehow to be a part of it all. She got no argument from us. In fact, we had just been commenting on her ability to lose herself for hours in the ridiculous time-suck that is the "EZ Bake Oven" app on her iPad.

Recognizing the opportunity to break myself of that nasty texting-and-driving habit, I suggested we also incorporate devices and apps (like Facebook and Twitter) into the mix. Since Alchemy didn't have access to these, she was cool with it.

So, here are the fast and not-so-loose ground rules for our Seven Day Media Cleanse: 1) No TV, 2) No apps, 3) No Internet. This meant no Facebook, Twitter, Netflix or Hulu and (voluntarily) included iTunes and streaming audio services (we use Beats).

For seven days, we listened to vinyl at home and had only work-related access to e-mail and Google Drive. We had dinner at the dining room table, said a short blessing before the meal, and enjoyed facing each other, talking and laughing. I endured deafening and cathartic silence on my morning and evening commute; my bag rode in the back seat. I rarely touched my phone, a stark contrast to the usual relationship I have with the device—a constant need to click and fondle, the straining of the eyes to scrutinize and decipher it's small type, and the panic when it's not immediately within reach. I was not exposed to any on-screen advertising; pop-up, in-line or e-mail notifications; marketing messages; in-app upgrade opportunities; pornographic images or news feeds.

To hear it told, you'd think I was an obsessive and domineering partner. But that's how we behave when we are fixated. That's how we act when we are addicted.

The effects of the cleanse were dramatic and the benefits were clear—I was calmer, more level-headed, more focused, less prone to distraction and, in the last couple days, felt a palpable happiness that was like a warmth throughout my body. I got current with my family and was more conversational with strangers.

Going forward, a media cleanse should be considered a serious part of our regular sacred fasting traditions (Lent, Ramadan, Maha Shivaratri). As with any dietary cleanse, the conditions are not universal, and it would not be the same (nor necessarily recommended) for everyone. However, the results consistently indicate that a more routine management of exposure to these types of media continues to yield significant benefits—including stress reduction, increased productivity, heightened overall well-being and, most importantly, a sense of actual connectedness to those around us.

Like any tool or prosthetic, if we allow the virtual web and our various devices to be a substitute for our own real hardware (body), software (mind) or GPS (soul), we risk confusing our partial experience of the Universe for the bigger picture. We risk confusing the technosphere with what Pierre Teilhard De Chardin called the "noösphere." And we risk the atrophy and loss of the latter for the former. Empathy, or the ability to feel subtle emotional and energetic shifts around us, will never develop as long as we are looking at a screen to find out how our friends and community are "feeling." Like the human bodies used as batteries in the film *The Matrix*, we risk being a "wet cell," plugged into a larger machine that relies on us to survive.

We risk never actually living ourselves. We risk everything.

Now, It's Your Turn

Are you interested in organizing or participating in a group media cleanse? Are you interested in cutting down your device (or social media) time, but not committing to a full seven days or more?

Try these tips to break you of your old habits.

1. **Get some distance.** Charge your phone across the room at night— don't be tempted to check any feeds before you're fully awake. Place your phone out of reach while driving—either in the back seat or trunk. Try silence on the car radio and see how it feels.

2. **Put your phone away when you're eating.** If you're with someone who is constantly checking updates on their phone, simply look them in the eye and initiate some conversation.

3. **Go hands-free!** Use a headset when on the phone. The less you

touch and fondle the device, the more you will reduce your compulsive and tactile attachment to it. And some argue that it's just plain healthier.

4. **Disrupt Your Routine.** Remove links and shortcuts to sites like Facebook and Twitter from your bookmarks and favorites. Keep a tally of the amount of times you unconsciously try to click on something that's no longer there.

If the idea of a cleanse or fast seems too radical or drastic for you, then simply try to be more aware of your behavior involving these screens, devices, apps, and software. By constantly **weeding** and **pruning** your apps, newsletters, feeds, network, (and yes, even friends), you are engaging in a conscious personal development. You are developing a higher and more acute level of "**infotention**" (a word penned by futurist Howard Rheingold). And you are affirming that you are no longer the same person you were when you subscribed to the "Southern Women's Turkey Meatball Recipes" e-newsletter back in 2011.

1. **Unsubscribe** to any e-newsletters that have become irrelevant or impractical. Don't passively mark them as spam or delete them. Actively unsubscribe.

2. **Unfollow** any people, brands, personalities, or accounts that you no longer enjoy or find authentic. People change, inside and out. And your favorites, lists, and feeds are a direct reflection of you, your tastes, and interests. Delete and deny access to any unused or extraneous apps that you have allowed access to your social media accounts.

3. **Unfriend.** That's right, I said it. I don't care if they're family. If that cousin of yours and his political or religious views are causing you undue stress or distraction, unfriend him. You'll still be related by blood, and you can still pick up the phone if you need to tell him you love him.

Be present, do the work. and move on.

Joran Slane Oppelt is a blogger, musician, interfaith minister, marketer, chaplain, public speaker, father, event producer, husband and facilitator – not necessarily in that order. Joran is the founder of the Integral Church in St. Petersburg, FL, and has spoken at many colleges and conferences including South by Southwest in Austin, TX. Integral Church is an interfaith community that encourages individuals to create their own personal transformative practice, using the tools and teachings from the world's major wisdom traditions in a pluralistic and sacred environment. For more information, follow @joranslane on Twitter or visit integralchurch.org.

Walking the Path: Your Spirit's Call

By Elizabeth Egan

Have you ever found yourself caught somewhere between the life you had and the life you want? Many times, transformation calls to us, but it is difficult to know just what steps to take toward the life that awaits. You may find you wake up one day completely unhappy with one of the major facets of your life, or the process may happen more gradually. Either way, it may be challenging to understand how to walk gracefully from the life you made for yourself in the past, to the life you want to make for yourself in the future.

Luckily, there are many things you can do to manifest a life that is in better vibrational harmony with the energy of your spirit, but first it is essential to discover who you truly are. If you do not know who you are at a core level, your ambitions will be of your ego instead of your Soul. Therefore, the first step in becoming more true to your authentic Self is to "know thyself" and to beware of false ambitions.

To accomplish this, you must first take an inventory of your talents, gifts, and dreams. Often, they are the language in which your Soul has chosen to expresses itself. False ambitions stem from wanting to feel secure, wanting to make others happy, or wanting to relieve the mind of stress and fear of lack. If you are doing something because you think it makes logical sense, but it goes against your nature, stop and ask yourself if this step is what you truly want at a Soul level. If you are unsure, set aside some time for solitude and contemplation. Think about the options available, and see what sensations come to your physical body. If there is any discomfort, pain or anxiety (especially in the solar plexus) then that is a strong indicator that your Soul is not in agreement with that decision. Eventually your Soul will have its way with you, and if you do not choose wisely at first, you will find yourself in the midst of deep transformation once again. There is no shame in this, however. For everything in life contributes toward our learning and evolving. It only matters that we honor the truth within.

After you come to know yourself, and you are sure that your ambitions are in alignment with your Soul's agenda for you, your next actions should fall under three main categories:

1. **Visualizing/Planning:** At this stage you are formulating your ideas for your true nature. During this stage, you may ask yourself questions such as....

   If I could do anything, what would it be?

   If I could go anywhere, where would I go?

   When I do _____time escapes me.

   I am happiest and most at peace when I _____.

   I feel most fulfilled and on purpose when I am_____.

   Most of us cannot simply jump from one life to another, but we can start small and act as if we already are who we wish to become. To do this, make a vision board or a Dream Box©, fill it with all the things you want to see and more importantly feel in your life. Do not obsess over it, however. Simply put it away, and let the Universe work its magic!

2. **Listening to and interpreting the whispers of Divine guidance:** The Universe is abundant with communication; we only need to learn how to interpret its language. Sometimes it seems we do not know which way to turn, but if we learn to depend on the whispers of Heaven and have faith, we will be more likely to achieve union with our highest states of self. Some things to keep in mind during this stage are:

   Remember to ask for guidance, and look for signs everywhere that the Universe is communicating with you — they may come in the form of books, songs, nature, conversations, numbers, etc. The Universe is unlimited, and it will communicate with you in unlimited ways.

   Look for signs that small dreams are coming true. Every time you notice life taking a step in the right direction, say a prayer of gratitude!

   Honor all Divine messages, and do not allow your mind to judge, criticize or worry about how things will unfold. Remember to be mindful that Divine intelligence is not limited by the confines of the human mind.

3. **Take Action!** Nothing shows the Universe you are serious about making changes than taking action. Some of the most efficient

ways of moving toward the life of your dreams include small things you can do to convince yourself that you are moving in the right direction.

Here are some suggestions:

Clutter clear! When you discard things that hold old energy, you also discard the energy. Nothing new can come to you unless you make the space for its arrival, so start making room for the new you to emerge!

Honor the moments when it is clearly time to take action, take a risk, or take a chance. These are the moments that hold within them the power to change your future!

Honor the visions you have for yourself and take small steps toward them. This may be as small as rearranging your desk, hanging up pictures, buying some new clothes, changing your hair style, whatever you need to do to "fit the part" of you in your new life. This becomes extremely important in getting the subconscious mind to work along with you.

Of course, these are just a few suggestions you can follow to manifest your personal transformation. However, by following these steps, you will be amazed how glimmers of your new life will start to show up. The Universe already knows how to make this happen for you…all you need to do is honor your Soul, visualize, listen, and have faith that with every step, the Divine walks alongside you.

Elizabeth Egan holds a Master's Degree in Education and has been a teacher in CT for 10 years. In addition, Elizabeth is also an accomplished spiritual singer, songwriter, and Reiki Master. She enjoys sharing her passion for transformation and mindfulness through her contributions to Transformation Magazine, teaching spiritual workshops, and her energy healing practice, Celtic Moon Reiki® where she gently blends the powers of sound and energy healing in order to harmonize and restore energetic balance to body, mind and spirit. Elizabeth released her first album, INSPIRED last spring, and is currently working on her first book, Gifts of Transformation. Contact eegan78@gmail.com.

Business as Transformation: From Being Employed to Becoming an Entrepreneur

By Linda Stewart

If you're one of the many people who dream of leaving your day job, quitting the rat race, and fulfilling your desire of being an entrepreneur this chapter is especially written for you.

Increasing numbers of successful professionals just like you have dreams and aspirations of breaking free from the restraints of the corporate world so that they can create the freedom and flexibility that comes from doing what they love and being their own boss. Often their dreams are fuelled by their desire to make a more meaningful contribution and have a bigger impact. They literally want to BE the change they want to see in the world.

Sadly, many postpone making good on their dreams and others will never progress beyond the dream. Why? Because they don't have a specific plan or know the exact steps they need to take to make it happen. In addition, they've likely fallen hostage to a variety of mainly fear-based reasons that they're allowing to get in the way: fear of failure, fear of success, fear of leaving the perceived security of a regular income and being able to provide for themselves, and their family. The list goes on.

However, by not taking action on your vision and making the contribution you dream of, you do yourself, your community, and ultimately the planet an immeasurable disservice. The truth is, those that make the leap quickly realize that "getting out of corporate" was one of the best decisions—if not the best decision—they ever made. With hindsight, they often wonder why they waited so darn long.

The best news is if you are committed, leaving the nine-to-five rat race and becoming a successful entrepreneur can happen much easier and much faster than you might think.

Below are just a few key steps and insights that can assist you to move forward with confidence and ultimately make the leap to creating the business and life you've so far only dreamed of.

Know Your Destination

The most important piece to actualizing your dream is to decide what it is you really want. Once you are clear about that you can bring your vision to life. You must have a crystal-clear vision of where you are going and exactly what you're trying to achieve. What are your specific long, medium and short-term goals?

If you need to generate an immediate modest income or if you want to build a multiple six- or seven-figure business, the steps you take will be completely different. Pinpoint where it is you're going so your subsequent actions will be in alignment with that. It will be much easier for you to confidently navigate towards your destination if you have more than just a vague idea. If you don't take the time to work out this crucial piece, you'll simply end up going nowhere fast.

Protect Your Dream

Refuse to let fear, self doubt, procrastination, lack of confidence, past experiences, money, other people's opinions, or anything else stop you from following your dream and living the life you truly desire. When you're ready to transform your life, none of these "excuses" will stop you. And if you are truly ready, you'll simply do what it takes and enlist the support and resources required to protect your dream and make it your reality.

You Don't Have To Be Perfect To Begin.

Avoid getting stuck in analysis paralysis, trying to get everything perfect before you begin. I've seen this many times in people making the transition from employee to entrepreneur where they're attempting to get all their ducks in a row before they begin. Resist the temptation to over analyze and instead begin now. And don't get caught up in busy work that offers no immediate return.

Building Your Business While Working Your Job

You can successfully build your business up part-time while still working in your job. That's exactly what one of my clients did. She successfully renegotiated her working hours providing additional scope for her to focus on her holistic practitioner training business. By her third month she was impacting more people's lives and generating more income than her full-time job. In this case, it allowed her to begin to build a contingency fund in savings, which made the transition to being a full-time business owner much easier and smoother. She is now fully self employed and has never looked back.

Open Your Mind to What Else is Possible

Think outside the conventional boxes about how you can leverage your time to help more people. One successful entrepreneur I know of has set up his location-independent business helping people live their dreams so that he now works just one hour a month and still generates multiple six figures while travelling and playing at the beach. He built a successful business — that helps hundreds of people around the world — around his most important value, spending quality time with his family. It's a fascinating example of a freedom-based portable business and a glimpse into what's actually possible.

The No. 1 Thing You Must Do to Leave Your Job in Record Time

You can go as fast or as slow as you choose with your business, but if you want to leave your job in record time you must focus first and foremost on income-producing activities. When I first started my boutique consultancy business for professional women and entrepreneurs, it took a mindset shift, picking up the phone and actually speaking with potential clients. Just two phone calls later I had two new consultancy clients and had actually banked more money than if I had worked for a whole month at my previous full-time job. And the truth is, it wasn't difficult.

I guarantee that you have at least one skill, more likely several, that you can put to work right away to generate an immediate income. So stop being busy, identify and get focused on the activities that will create momentum in your emerging business and catapult you out of employment and into entrepreneurship.

LINDA STEWART BSc is a #1 bestselling author, executive consultant and facilitator of transformational events for discerning professional & entrepreneurial women. From her home in the tropics of South East Asia, she runs a number of 'portable' location-independent businesses. Linda passionately champions and empowers her worldwide clientele to replicate the 'portable business model' in order to create their own sustainable businesses — marrying up what they love and living life on their own terms. Through her work with collaborative partners and her own business and lifestyle consulting expertise, she offers her international clientèle access to exclusive tropical transformational retreats, and networking opportunities at intimate events for women professionals & entrepreneurs. Visit www.ThePortableBusinessCoach.com.

SECTION VII:
LOVE AND RELATIONSHIPS

Healing from Toxic Relationships

By Tracey Ashcraft

When we think of toxic relationships, our focus usually turns to romance. However, these caustic bonds can solidify in many areas of our lives: between parents and children, relatives, coworkers, friends, and even members of groups. Admitting that a relationship is unhealthy can be difficult, especially if it revolves around a long-term commitment (such as marriage) or a family tie. We often turn the other cheek and ignore the red flags and warning signs—until we end up feeling like we are backed into a corner. We may then go on the defensive, adding more negative fuel to the fire in the form of resentment and fear.

By the time you realize that you are in a toxic relationship, you most likely feel defeated, confused, angry and beaten down. The patterns of behavior you have employed to cope with the unpredictable and unsettling behaviors of a toxic partner have become entrenched, such as pleasing, shaping your actions to avoid the wrath of the next temper tantrum, and walking on "eggshells." Sadly these tactics do not work to change the unsavory behaviors of the toxic person in your life nor do they make you happy long-term. However, there are seven steps that *you* can take to truly begin to break the patterns and survive a toxic relationship:

Step 1: Realize that you cannot change anyone but yourself.

You may find yourself thinking, "If she would just talk to a counselor things would be better." Or, "If he would just ask me for what he wants then he wouldn't have to manipulate me." No amount of convincing, wishing or hoping will change another person. He or she must want to change and realize that his/her coping skills are not working. Accept that you are the only one you can change.

Step 2: Stop trying to please everyone.

Stop trying to be liked. Those who end up in toxic relationships tend to put the needs of others first. People pleasers often have endured childhood neglect or were led to believe that other's needs were more important than their needs. Love may have been conditional, or it may have felt like love needed to be earned. In healthy relationships love is unconditional. It does not come with a price tag. Does this sound like you?

Once you let go of trying to earn approval, things begin to shift. You will feel more empowered. The toxic person may ramp up more at first, so it is important to stick with these steps. Regardless of how the other person behaves, you will feel better when you are bringing your power back inside yourself.

Step 3: Quit taking it personally.

The other party's tirades are not about you. You didn't cause that person's pain—even if he or she tells you that you did. This step ties into Step 2. Once you stop trying to be liked or accepted, it will matter less what others think of you. When someone criticizes you or blames you unjustly, you will not feel the need to defend. When you stop taking it personally and realize it is not about you, you will be taking a huge step toward freeing yourself from pain!

When you are feeling attacked in a toxic relationship say to yourself, "It's not about me." Write this phrase on a small card and carry it with you in your purse or wallet. Practice saying it daily as an affirmation.

Step 4: Take steps to believe in yourself.

When you start to believe that you are good enough just as you are, you will be able to realize that the avalanche of negativity that comes your way is not really about you. Surround yourself with people who believe in you. Write a list of the good qualities you possess. Add to it each day. Remember you are not perfect; you are perfectly fine just as you are.

Step 5: Set and maintain healthy boundaries.

Boundary setting is not selfish or mean, even if it is perceived that way. When setting boundaries, you can let the person know that you respect his or her wishes but also will be taking care of yourself.

For example: If your toxic partner demands you listen when you are in bed trying to sleep, you can say: "I will be happy to listen to you after breakfast when I am rested and can be fully present for you." If he or she keeps pushing, become a broken record. Repeat your boundary and do not give in. Remember to stick to the boundaries even when you feel like your partner will like you less than when you are in people-pleaser mode.

Step 6: Find a style of meditation that will help you on this journey.

It is important to have some form of daily ritual to relax your mind and spirit. For some it may be doing yoga. For others it may be taking a daily walk. If you walk with a friend, make sure that you limit the negative talk of drama in your life. Try sitting outside somewhere that you find peaceful and spend at least 10 minutes noticing what you see around you. Notice the sights, sounds and smells. Carving out this daily relaxation time for yourself actually helps you to resist getting sucked into the vortex of negativity you may experience from a toxic person in your life.

Step 7: Seek help from a professional who understands toxic relationships.

Dealing with the unpredictable behaviors and poor coping skills of a toxic person on a daily basis can really take a heavy toll on your overall well-being. You can become isolated and fearful of talking about the problem. A professional on your team can help speed the healing process and keep you motivated when you feel like throwing in the towel. Look for someone who has experience with personality disorders and who understands toxic relationships.

Remember that the process of recovering from the drama of a toxic relationship takes time. It is a healing journey and there is no quick fix. For true success, you need to learn that you *are* good enough and that you do not need the approval of others to know that you are!

Tracey Ashcraft, MA, LPC, is a licensed professional counselor, confidence coach, and entrepreneur. After 10 years as an award-winning sales representative, she earned her Master's in Counseling from Regis University in Denver, CO. Tracey founded Best Life Therapy in 2004, a practice specializing in helping adults and college students to heal from toxic relationships. Tracey offers a down-to-earth-tell-it-like-it-is, sometimes humorous approach that helps clients create a life they are excited to live. She is a regular contributor to Transformation Magazine and creator of the JerseyGirlGuide.com website and blog. Counseling sessions are available to individuals and couples in Boulder, CO, and coaching sessions are available via phone and video conferencing. To learn more visit BestLifeTherapy.com.

Mama Drama Trauma:
How to Forgive and Stop Living It

By Tammy Taylor

"To have a serious illness or injury is difficult enough; seeing it as a punishment or the cruel caprice of fate only makes it harder to bear." — Caroline Myss, medical intuitive, author, mystic

Soul alignment is when the ego chooses to yield its life to the soul before its physical death. Living a soul-aligned life has transformed me from an emotionally abandoned daughter — someone who lived in a constant state of hysteria — into a spiritual growth life coach fulfilling my soul contract to empower others to heal from the damaging effects of Mama Drama Trauma.

"Mama Drama Trauma" (MDT) is a condition by which the mother inflicts unhealed aspects of herself onto her children causing physical and/or emotional trauma. In extreme cases where the mother is unable, unwilling, or unavailable to heal, loving detachment is not an option — it is the last resort for MDT suffers to live a happy and healthy life.

Doing so through "Loving Detachment", the process I am about to share, is the most powerful thing I've ever done. It is not about trying to rid our mother from our lives; it's about consciously staying soul connected.

MDT is a clarion call to reframe our story, drop the drama, and recommit to our soul journey. The Spiritual lesson of this experience for soul is to learn how to unconditionally love and nurture itself. If ego chooses to co-creatively assist, soul evolves and ego heals.

Loving detachment allows us to see all this clearly and objectively. It diffuses the emotional tyranny of MDT by providing the time and space we need to transcend the demands of an unhealthy ego that insists we are nothing more than our biography.

How MDT Affects Us

Dr. Norman Shealy, neurosurgeon and pain medicine pioneer, says, "Children who feel unloved either become depressed or juvenile delinquents, and depressed and socially delinquent children tend to become depressed and/or delinquent adults."

It is a ravenous cycle.

MDT kills. MDT steals. MDT famously makes life hell on wheels.

Here are the telltale signs you may have MDT:

- You struggle to make decisions on your own because you need constant approval.
- Your feelings are easily hurt, and you are convinced everything people say and do is about you.
- You have self-sabotaging inner dialogue and self-destructive addictions.
- You have a one-sided relationship with your mother because you don't feel heard.
- Your entire identity is based on how much others, particularly your mother, value you.
- You project your own feelings of insecurity onto others, harshly judging those you don't like and attracting emotionally insecure friends.
- No matter what you do, you feel out of sync with the world around you (You find it impossible to "be present".)
- Your life is lonely.
- The act is tired; you're sick and tired of being sick and tired and out of moves.

You don't know what to do, but there's only one thing left to do...admit it: You suffer from MDT (or the closely related PDT, Papa Drama Trauma).

How to Heal MDT

Two practices healed my MDT: soul alignment and sacred alignment. Soul alignment is yielding ego identity, biography, and conditioning to one's intuitive guidance and the unceasing love and appreciation soul has for us. Sacred alignment is soul alignment between two or more souls cooperatively fulfilling their soul contract.

Dr. Norm Shealy and Carolyn Myss teach the science of medical intuition, and assess our soul mates as those who cause the greatest pain in our lives. As a Baptist born Midwesterner, learning to see my mother from this perspective threw me into decade long research about love, soul, Spirit, and how to reclaim my personal power.

The Ritual of Loving Detachment in 5 Steps

Rituals are rites of passage to soul and sacred alignment. The crucial role addiction plays in MDT directly correlates to the absence of ritual in our lives. We need ritual to transition, transform, accept, and release what no longer serves the personal and collective consciousness. Carrying MDT and other such personal and social burdens of the past impede progression on our evolutionary path until they are ritualized.

Loving Detachment, like all rituals, is catharsis in three rites: separation, transformation, and integration.

The first initiation is when we ACKNOWLEDGE THE WOUND of truth of our MDT experience by trusting our intuition, releasing denial, and separating from the drama to soul align. We ASK "IS IT TRUE?" Did mama abuse, abandon, not love me? We amp up meditation and prayer. We ultimately get clarity about the crisis and the anger through inquiry and observation of how we allow MDT to define us and our lives.

In the last phase of separation, we PROCESS THE TRUTH shifting from our ego to soul perspective of the mother.

In the next rite of transformation, we are REBORN. By asserting self acceptance, bold acts of creative expression, play, and self-nurturing habits we detox victimhood. At this stage, sacred alignment begins in earnest as we consciously choose to interact with individuals, situations, and memories in ways to resolve drama and heal unfinished trauma.

Finally, through integration, actually living the Reality we are never alone, or unloved even when we feel unmothered, we LIBERATE ourselves to fully live in soul alignment, remaining connected with whom we are beyond this incarnation with sincerity, love, forgiveness and compassion.

Healing a Human Disorder

MDT is the planet's biggest taboo. Its affects are as universal as motherhood, so until we heal it, we will continue to project the same unloving thoughts, behaviors, and beliefs onto ourselves and others.

When we can see the drama as something to which we as mother/child/soul mates agreed to experience, to keep us both on our evolutionary track, then what formerly seemed like an arbitrary or even absurd situation can be seen for what it is, a significant lesson on our soul journey.

Detachment from mama to heal MDT is not a forever proposition. It is as long as it takes to heal from its emotional triggers to gain sure footing in soul alignment and self love.

Mama may never change, but there is nothing is more transformative than the ability to "BE and Speak Your Truth With Love!"

Tammy Taylor has one job: to show people how to forgive and stop living Mama Drama Trauma (MDT). In 2012, Tammy's world as a life coach was turned upside down when she detached from her emotionally abusive mother. Within two years, her self-talk, relationships, and coaching practice transformed through a soul guided process she calls "Loving Detachment". Her sound therapy, books, videos, public events, retreats and private sessions bring the freedom to "BE and Speak Your Truth With Love" to people all over the world. Tammy's highly anticipated book, *Mama Drama Trauma: How to Forgive and Stop Living It* is due early 2015. Visit www.MamaDramaTrauma.com.

Send Love Ahead

By Noelle Sterne

Darcy came into the Bible study group looking radiant, happier than I'd ever seen her. She couldn't wait to tell us what had happened. The previous week, she'd been worriedly repeating the details of the upcoming custody hearing for her daughter. After Darcy's recent divorce, her husband was attempting to undermine her character to sway the judge for custody.

But now, Darcy was transformed. Maybe, more accurately, *triumphant*. The hearing was very short, she said, and the judge saw through her husband's tactics. Darcy was awarded custody and at the end, to her astonishment, her husband turned to her and said, "It's probably for the best."

The group members congratulated Darcy and shared her joy. Two of us commented on the astounding change in her. "What caused it?" we asked. She told us of a process she'd discovered for meeting challenges like these that stemmed from her study of *A Course in Miracles*.

Darcy called it "Send Love Ahead." She described how it works and, at the next group meeting, gave us all a typed summary of her meditative method. Here it is.

1. Sit quietly apart from everything.
2. Close your eyes and take some slow, deep breaths.
3. Visualize the event that fills you with dismay. See the room or setting, where you'll be appearing, working, sitting, talking. If you don't know the specifics literally, imagine them.
4. If you've been resisting the situation ("I *wish* I didn't have to do this!"), admit it. Rage if you must.
5. If you're afraid, admit that too. Darcy said that she was so fearful in the days before the hearing that she couldn't eat and shouted out loud at home, "I'm afraid!" Often when you admit it fully, it dissipates.
6. Do your homework. If it's a presentation, speech, or call, write it out.
7. If you need to, research the contents. If it's a written or other

creative project, list the steps necessary to complete it. If it's a defense of something, make notes and practice your points. Darcy wrote out all the positive reasons she should be awarded custody (and without maligning her ex-husband).

8. Mentally go back to the place or situation, whether it's an office, auditorium, meeting room, judge's chambers, or your own study. Fill the physical space with love.

9. See the room shining in light.

10. Picture yourself and ever other person involved smiling, extending hands to you, nodding "Yes."

11. Feel the light and peace envelop you and radiate out from you.

12. Gently think about how you want to emerge from the situation. See yourself afterwards in a favorite, comfortable and comforting environment, like a reward.

13. Think about how you want to feel after it's over. How do you really want to feel? What do you want to have accomplished or settled? What direction do you want to know you're next going in?

14. Write down your answers to these questions. Writing them down is stating your affirmations. Record as many specifics as you can. Don't be shy or modest. You *deserve* all the rewards and blessed outcomes.

15. See every other person involved leaving feeling satisfied, fulfilled, happy with the outcome, and ready to take the next constructive action.

16. Say to yourself: "I surrender all to God. I feel only Love here."

17. Repeat these words every time you feel anxious about the situation or tempted to visualize something less than perfect.

18. Sit quietly feeling this Love.

19. Practice these steps twice a day.

My Own Experience

A week after Darcy told the group about this method, I had the opportunity to test it. In a few days, I had to attend a difficult meeting on behalf of a client. Using Darcy's principles and steps, beforehand I prepared the materials necessary, practiced my opening statement aloud and in an increasingly firm voice. Then, several times a day, I visualized the office where the meeting would take place. I saw it and everyone in it filled with Love, illumined. I projected Love to each person I knew would be there.

I made a list of how I wanted to feel afterwards. My adjectives included "knowledgeable," "reasonable," "professional," "peaceful," "strong," "satisfied with the outcome," "understood," respected," "listened to," "having accomplished the task," "achieved the perfect administrative decision for my client," "knowing the next direction."

I visualized too relating the positive outcome to my client, and both of us congratulating each other. On the day of the meeting, as I drove, I kept saying "Love is here."

Yes, I was nervous, hands clammy, stomach feeling hollow. But I knew I'd prepared, practically and spiritually. My hands gradually warmed and my stomach stabilized as I repeated "Love is here."

The meeting started on time and went smoothly. I said what I had to, listened attentively to the others, and responded in even tones. Afterwards, driving home, I glanced at my list. To what shouldn't have been my amazement, every one of those positive outcomes had been fulfilled. And more—the individuals on the other side assured me of their complete cooperation to resolve the matter speedily. I felt great gratitude—to Darcy, to the *Course in Miracles*, and to the Creator.

When I related my experience at the next group meeting, one of the members referred us to Lesson 349 in the *Course in Miracles Workbook*, and I recommend it for similar situations:

> *Today I let Christ's vision look upon*
> *All things for me and judge them not, but give*
> *Each one a miracle of love instead.*

In any difficult situation you may face, especially one you want to run and hide from, think about this lesson and Darcy's steps. Use them before a thorny phone call, a meeting you dread, an exam you're scared of, a project you don't know how to start, a presentation that terrifies you, a creative session you cringe at plunging into.

Sit quietly, take a few deep breaths, do your homework, and visualize the absolute best outcomes. You deserve all of them—as you send love ahead.

Noelle Sterne, Ph.D., author, editor, coach, and spiritual counselor, publishes widely in print and online venues, including Children's Book Insider, Funds for Writers, Inspire Me Today, Transformation Magazine, Unity Magazine, Writer's Digest, The Writer, and Author Magazine's "Authors' Blog." With a Ph.D. from Columbia University, Noelle assists doctoral candidates as they complete their dissertations. Her forthcoming book is *Challenges in Writing Your Dissertation: Coping with the Emotional, Interpersonal, and Spiritual Struggles*. In Noelle's first book *Trust Your Life: Forgive Yourself and Go After Your Dreams* (Unity Books, 2011), she helps readers release regrets, re-label their past, and reach lifelong yearnings. Visit www.trustyourlifenow.com.

Transforming Divorce

By Dr. Marty Finkelstein

"I want a divorce" were the words that began a journey of pain, anger, and sadness that I did not want to take. It was a journey that evoked fears of the future and loss. It riddled me with denial and confusion, and poked a hot branding iron into my heart, unleashing unwanted rage. Thankfully, it was also a journey of healing, discovery, and vulnerability that ultimately led to forgiveness and love.

These types of journeys can only be taken alone. Even with the best intentions on the part of family and friends, inevitably we are on our own to make decisions affecting our relationships.

The words "I want a divorce," etched their way deep into my muscles and blood and, like a cancer, they were rapidly taking over my body. I sat frozen for hours feeling like a victim, though truly I was not. My feelings were the result of having neglected the ongoing symptoms of an illness, symptoms that are simple to recognize when we are "awake."

The harmony of the relationship that once existed was out of tune. Where there was once affection and healthy communication, now there was judgment and isolation. Where there was once open-heartedness and trusting, now there was a feeling of being guarded and contracted. Where there was once mutual admiration and sexual intimacy, now there was awkwardness and hopelessness. My partner and I once shared a mutual vision regarding family, careers, and spiritual development. Now the vision was clouded. Sadly, when we are sleepwalking through a relationship, symptoms are rationalized through denial and illusions, until abruptly awakened.

As I began a journey of inner healing and looking deeply within, I observed there had been one constant factor in all my relationships—me. I discovered how, to some degree, I had sabotaged all of my intimate romantic relationships. Somehow I would subconsciously manifest each relationship ending by the other person leaving me. Perhaps initially it was the fear of deeper intimacy and commitment on my part. But, ultimately it also was that I did not want to be the one who chose to leave the relationship. Because I did not feel that I deserved to be loved for who I was, I held back my own love and vulnerability.

How do we get to this horrible place? It is certainly not our intention to eventually divorce when we first fall in love and decide to get married. Hopefully, we anticipate our marriage will last forever. Yet more marriages are failing, more divorces are occurring, and more children are being raised without the loving support of a mom and dad living together. How do we slip out of love and fall from grace with our partner? My own experience tells me it is quite easy. It is as easy as accepting illness as a normal state of health as we age. We enter relationships as if we already know what to do to manifest a wonderful, lifelong partnership. Yet who have been our role models for healthy, passionate, understanding relationships?

Perhaps you have been fortunate to have witnessed a mom and dad display loving, respectful qualities your whole life. But for most of us, our idea of romance and partnering has come from television, movies, and the not-so-perfect role models within our communities. The truth is we have to learn how to cultivate relationships and see them as a mirror of our own desire to evolve emotionally and spiritually. We have to learn to respect our partner even when we may be in disagreement or feeling stressed. We have to take the time to communicate with each other and learn to listen compassionately. We have to learn that it is all right to be angry sometimes, but it is not all right to take the anger out on our partner in a mean-spirited way. We have to learn how to be tender even when fatigued and how to forgive and understand that broken promises take time to heal. Marriage works when two people continually strive to grow together, share visions and dreams, and honor, respect, appreciate, and trust each other along the way.

The Healing Process

There are many stages in the process of healing, though the first is often motivated by the instinct to survive. But survival simply keeps us stuck battling in the war that can poison our life forever. When I reflect on my own divorce, there was one moment that created a healing shift, a transformation. It was a moment of rage and anger that took control of my body. It brought me to my knees as I looked into a future of fighting over our children, finances, and child support and knowing our lives would suffer the consequences.

I felt helpless, my intellect and wisdom were no longer to be found. I closed my eyes and drifted into a meditation, calling upon God for help. "I don't know the answer. I need your guidance." I repeated it like a mantra. I had asked for guidance before, but this time I was truly on my knees because I couldn't stand without shaking. I had always had a relationship with a higher power since I was a child. It came naturally to me. It didn't feel religious, just true. Sometimes God answered, and sometimes there was the understanding that God works in mysterious ways. But this time I heard an answer, and I didn't have to wait long. The answer was precise and clear with no room to misunderstand the message: *In your deepest rage and anger you will discover deeper love, wisdom, and compassion, and when you do, you will want to share that healing gift with others.*

I had been feeling the rage of a hurricane, but at that moment I felt waves of peace flow through me as things became crystal clear. There was only one person I could change and that was me. I didn't know what the future would hold but, at that instant, I knew I was going to bring compassion, love, forgiveness, and peace to my family.

People often ask me, "How do I stop repeating the cycle of painful relationships? How do I keep myself from becoming bitter and disenchanted?" When we learn the healing lessons, our heart continues to open to greater love, forgiveness, and compassion. In essence, we all must learn to give what we truly want. If you want love, give love. If you want healthy communication, practice healthy communication. If you desire passion and tenderness, give passion and tenderness. Learn to listen to the voice within.

If you are going through a divorce, begin to write out a vision of how you would desire your life to look in two years. Imagine your life being fully expressed and extraordinary in the areas of your family, your new relationships, career, finances, children, and your own emotional, physical and spiritual wellness. Begin the healing journey by enrolling in seminars, and workshops with the willingness to learn about the most important person in your life; you!

Dr. Marty Finkelstein has been a holistic chiropractor for over thirty years. He is the author of several books including: *DIVORCE: An Uncommon Love Story, IF RELATIONSHIPS WERE LIKE SPORTS, MEN WOULD AT LEAST KNOW THE SCORE, THE SEVEN GIFTS, A LIFE OF WELLNESS,* and *8 LESSONS FOR LIFE ON HOLE 1.* He is an innovative speaker and teacher who empowers people to greater wellness and healing in their lives, and created and leads the seminars. Dr. Marty plays guitar and ukulele, and has a CD called MOMENTS IN TIME. He is excellent friends with his ex-wife and parenting partners for their two children. He is in a relationship with his soul mate and sweetheart and lives in Decatur, GA. Visit www.mydecaturchiropractor.com.

SECTION VIII:
SPIRITUAL AWAKENING

It's All B.S.

By Gregg Sanderson

"A belief system is just a thought you keep thinking." –
Abraham-Hicks

From militant Atheism to the strictest Fundamentalism, from radical vegan to raving carnivore, from Socialist to Libertarian, we are run by our belief systems. They influence everything from sex, religion, and politics to life itself, before, during, and after.

With all the conflicting belief systems in the world, how can we tell which ones work? Here's the big secret. They all do.

Indeed, every belief creates its corresponding circumstance. The more restrictive our beliefs, the more restricted our lives. For the purpose of instructive abbreviation, I will use the initials of Belief System throughout.

If my B.S. says, "Life is difficult," I struggle without satisfaction.
If my B.S. says, "I'm a guilty sinner," I live in wretchedness and remorse.
If my B.S. says, "Poverty is a virtue," I spend a lot of time broke or guilty.
If my B.S. says, "There's not enough," I never stop looking for more.
If my B.S. says, "It's cold and flu season," I know just when to sneeze.
If my B.S. says, "I'm born to suffer," my happiness comes with guilt.
If my B.S. says, "I'll never love again," I create my own loneliness.
If my B.S. says ,"I'm not worthy," I live life as a loser.

Are you getting the instructive part of the abbreviation?

Suppose instead:

My B.S. says, "Life is easy," I might not kill myself working.
My B.S. says, "Not guilty," I could live in innocence.
My B.S. says, "It's good to be rich," it would be OK to have lots of money.
My B.S. says, "Life is abundant," I'd reap the bounty.
My B.S. says, "Joy is my birthright," I wouldn't need misery.
My B.S. says, "Perfect health is natural," I'd swallow fewer pills.
My B.S. says, "Love is all around," I'd live in ecstasy.
My B.S. says, "I deserve the best," I'd enjoy it more.

Some B.S.es are better than others, but they're still B.S.

You may argue this point. You may say, "I believe in prosperity, but I'm still broke." Or, "I went to a relationship seminar, but I'm still a jerk." Or, "I eat the right foods and do healthy stuff, but I'm still sick."

If you want a clue as to why such beliefs aren't working, remember the quote at the beginning of this chapter: "A belief system is just a thought you keep thinking." No matter what you say, if you keep thinking broke, jerk, or sick your words won't mean much. Five minutes of nice words won't be enough to counter 23 hours and 55 minutes of the opposite belief.

This book offers more B.S.—other ways to picture life and the Universe that make sense or not, depending upon your B.S. If your B.S. is B.S., what have you got to lose by living with THIS B.S.? It's all B.S. anyhow, so you might as well have fun with it.

Yet it doesn't take any B.S. to scratch my nose. It itches, I scratch. That's how it works. That's how the Universe works, too…no matter what your B.S.

Science can't prove (or disprove) a Spiritual activity. Science is but one facet of the Spiritual Universe, and confined to the space/time continuum. By definition, it can't consider dimensions that don't exist on this plane, so we can't properly turn to science to explain Spiritual matters. The Scientific Method is the accepted procedure for discovery. Generally it has four steps:

1. Observation and description of a phenomenon or group of phenomena.
2. Formulation of a hypothesis to explain the phenomena.
3. Use of the hypothesis to predict the existence of other phenomena, or to predict quantitatively the results of new observations.
4. Performance of experimental tests of the predictions by independent experimenters and properly performed experiments.

What a bunch of gobbledegook!

Wouldn't it be great if words could never have more than two syllables? Well, maybe not, since "syllables" has three. Let's apply the scientific method:

1. I observe that a sentence only has two-syllable words.
2. I hypothesize that words only have two syllables or less.
3. I write another sentence and find some of the words have more than two syllables.
4. Other people write sentences with polysyllables.

Thus, I have disproved the hypothesis. Back to the ole drawing board. Now, let's get real.

- I observe that my thoughts create my experience.
- I suggest that thought is creative.
- I think some other thoughts and nothing happens.

- Other people think thoughts and wonder what happened.
- Thus, I have disproved the hypothesis...Or have I?

Look:

> *The Secret* works often enough for somebody to write a book about it.
> *Science of Mind* " " " " " " " " " " "
> *Psychic Healing* " " " " " " " " " " " "
> *Spiritualism* " " " " " " " " " " " "
> *Channeling* " " " " " " " " " " "
> And *Science* " " " " " " " " " " "

So what's going on? I'll tell you.

I don't know.

One thing is for sure, neither does Science. While they make fascinating discoveries, who knows the myriad of dimensions in the Universe completely imperceptible to us limited Space/Time adventurers.

Meanwhile, the best we can do is to be content with empirical evidence. We see or experience the B.S. enough so that it's valid to adopt. For example, I know that manifestation requires consistent embodied thought powered by emotion with a mix of gratitude...But there's no way to measure embodiment, emotion, how strong the belief, how regular the thought, or even the results.

So it works when it works, and it doesn't when it doesn't, and if it works often enough I'll adopt it as my own B.S.

There are too many variables in the metaphysical world that don't lend themselves to objective measurement, which makes the scientific method of limited value. For example, could anybody measure and control the receptivity to intuitive guidance—or the validity? Of course not.

What it boils down to is, if a Spiritual Trip works for you, stick with it. If not, find something else. They all work as long as you believe in them. Of course, first you have to believe that they work as long as you believe in them.

Gregg Sanderson studied a variety of spiritual teachings before he became a licensed practitioner in the Centers For Spiritual Living and a Certified Trainer/Trailblazer for Infinite Possibilities. He is a speaker and workshop facilitator who has worked with thousands of individuals and couples using the Science of Happiness. Gregg authored *What Ever Happened To Happily Ever After?*, *Split Happens – Easing the Pain of Divorce*, and *Spirit With A Smile – The World According To BOB*. He is co-creator of the New Thought Global Network (www.newthoughtglobal. org), an on-line living collection of inspirational outpouring, designed to deliver New Thought teachings virtually. Contact gregg@newthoughtglobal.org.

Who Said That?

By Linda Commito

We learn a lot about our world through our five senses, yet we often take them for granted, only realizing their value when they diminish with age or we lose one of them. What we are less likely to acknowledge is that we comprehend and experience life with more than sight, hearing, smell, taste and touch, and that oftentimes our less-tangible senses are far more effective than their physical counterparts.

For example, do you sometimes seem to just *know* things? We may not always be able to put a name to it or explain *how* we know, we just do. Even scientists can't explain the reasons behind the feelings and perceptions of someone who is in touch with their intuition, their inner wisdom and guidance system.

We may understand things about people that have nothing to do with what they are saying or doing. We know how we feel when we walk away from someone and we're able to cut through the social politeness to get to the essence of what just transpired. We oftentimes base our trust of others more on the good vibes or feelings that we get from them than by the words they speak.

We are just beginning to realize the power of our thoughts and how interconnected everything is. We think about someone and moments later they call, saying, "You were just on my mind." Even though this is a common phenomenon today, it is still strong validation that a world exists beyond our physical senses.

This type of communication happens with beings outside of our physical environment too. We can ask for the help that we need and we can tune in to our angels or guides, who are ready to assist us if we allow it. And if we are really listening, what we hear can offer tremendous support and can even save lives.

Clear Messages

There have been several instances in my own life when I've received clear messages, sometimes through a dream and other times through a *voice*. I've learned the importance of being open to these messages and to respond immediately.

One July 4th weekend, at dusk, I was driving to the mountains in my four-wheel drive vehicle, which was filled with food, clothes and my big German shepherd. Since I don't drive well in the dark and was eager to get to my weekend destination, I was driving faster than I should have been in the passing lane on a busy highway.

Suddenly, seemingly out of nowhere, I heard a voice: "Slow down and move into the right lane." I responded immediately and moved over into the next lane just as my right rear tire exploded and shredded into pieces. Because I'd reduced my speed, I was able to safely move over to the shoulder of the highway and stop the car. I was shocked, realizing that if this had happened just moments before, I could have been seriously injured or killed.

I believe, too, that sometimes people who show up in our life at just the right time have also heard and listened to a "voice," following an instinct to do something that is not usually a part of their routine. After my tire blew out, without a cell phone and with no houses or highway exit nearby, I watched the sky getting darker as I wondered how I was going to get to my destination. I had stood by the side of my vehicle for about 15 minutes when a Safeway supermarket truck pulled up. A kind-hearted young man, who didn't normally stop on his work route, got out to offer his assistance, and I was soon safely on my way.

At times, that *voice* has saved lives. Two different people, at different times and locations, have told me almost identical stories. One friend, Amy (alias), said that she had gone to a party with two friends, leaving behind a roommate who didn't want to go with them. At one point, Amy was sitting alone at the party when she heard a voice say, "Go home!" *Who said that?* she wondered as she looked around, but there was no one nearby. Amy jumped up, gathered her friends, and headed home, where she found her roommate in critical condition from a suicidal overdose. They were able to rush her roommate to a hospital in time to save her life.

Kevin, a compassionate teen whom I spoke with recently, had a similar experience. He and a friend shared an apartment, but on this particular day Kevin was visiting with his dad. While he was at his dad's, he heard a clear voice tell him to "Go home!" At first he thought, *Well, I am home*, thinking of his dad's home as his. But without hesitating, Kevin told his dad that he had to go and drove to his apartment where he found his housemate writing a suicide note. Kevin invited him to go to the beach and just talk—heart to heart. There he shared with his friend his own experiences with despair and how he had turned his life around. It was a valuable conversation and today Kevin's friend is doing some good things with his life by helping others.

Messengers come in all shapes, forms, and sizes to convey meaningful information. We may see images, hear voices, or just have a feeling that something is not right, but the messages may be just what is needed to turn a life around, to save a life—whether it is ours, someone we love's, or a total stranger's. We may not know *who said that*, but when we hear that voice, it's enough to just pay attention.

Linda Commito, author, speaker, entrepreneur, consultant, and teacher, is passionate about her vision to leave this world a kinder, more loving, and interconnected place. Her award-winning book of inspirational stories, *Love is the New Currency*, demonstrates how we can each make an important difference in the lives of others through simple acts of love and kindness. Ms. Commito believes that in order to inspire a kinder world the place to start is with children. She volunteered at a Title One elementary school, working with over 500 students, to create "Kindness Starts With Me," a program, book, and web site for children. Please visit www.loveisthenewcurrency.com and www.kindnessstartswithme.com.

The Muddy Little Lotus

By Carol Hasbrouck

Sitting quietly, I am reminded
That life can sometimes be quite blinded.
Like a fist that is clenched so tight
Afraid and bound up with all its might.

But when relaxed and released, it may find
A freedom and joy, simple peace of mind.
A fist clenched so tight is like a flower
A lotus, perhaps, in its darkest hour.

All muddy and wet, with no light in sight
Being all bound up, it feels such a fright.
But the light, it knows, is always right there
It can't see it right now. It just doesn't dare.

Until the perfect time, the Light to arrive
For the muddy little lotus to again
come alive.
Then slowly it begins, it starts to
sprout forth
One petal at a time, it unfolds to move north.

Toward the bright light, always shining
from above
Spread out wide, with great wings, full
of love.
The once muddy flower begins to know
The darkness it felt was only a show.

It had to release, feel free and let go
For the light to enter and start to grow.

Once begun, there's no stopping the
unfolding.
The Great Light was waiting to begin
Its molding
Of the muddy little lotus into
something anew
A beautiful white flower sprouted, as
it grew.

Into a symbol of purity, divine birth
and perfection
A place for all Buddhas to gain
some reflection
Of the meaning of Life, Spirit and
True Love
The sacred space of knowing, shining
down from above.

You and I are like the little lotus, all
muddy and wet
Feeling scared and alone, bound up in
our fret
Until we release, surrender and let go
To the place always there, what we
already know.

Reflecting on the beautiful lotus flower each day reminds us to keep some perspective on our own life. Each morning, this symbol of divine purity and spiritual awakening emerges from its muddy, submerged resting place, unstained and unaffected by the darkness below. It shines brightly and radiates quintessential beauty for all to behold.

It is one of the most ancient and profound symbols of planet Earth. According to Egyptian myth, it is the Sun of creation and rebirth. In some parts of Asia it is the symbol of spiritual awakening and to Buddhists it represents good fortune. Buddha is often pictured sitting atop this magnificent flower. In Tantrism, the lotus represents the feminine principle and the Hindus believe the unfolding petals suggest the expansion of the soul.

The flower, like people, comes in a variety of colors, each with its own meaning. In Buddhism, the white lotus flower is a symbol of purity of mind and spirit. One of the most celebrated is the pink flower, considered sacred and associated with Buddha himself. A red lotus flower is connected with the heart and represents compassion and love. Blue flowers call forth wisdom, logic and common sense, all of which is needed to create enlightenment. The purple lotus can be depicted as an open flower or a bud and its eight petals are representative of the noble eightfold path; one of Buddha's principal teachings. It speaks of spirituality and mysticism. Lastly, the gold lotus flower represents the achievement of full enlightenment and self-awareness.

But, how does this muddy little flower benefit us in our daily reflections? As human beings, we live in a world of duality: up and down, hot and cold, good and bad, fear and love. Without the one, we can't know the meaning of the other. Not one of us can say our entire life has been one of joy or one of misery and pain. No one escapes this ever-pervasive duality on earth while being "of the world." At times we are muddy and wet, living in darkness and fear, while at other times we spread our wings and fly high on love and the light of joy.

The goal, the craving, the eternal desire inside each of us is to experience peace and joy in all situations.

How can the muddy little lotus show us the way? By remembering that the darkness always passes, the dirt, the mud, gets washed away, sometimes quickly, sometimes slowly. But it will always materialize, if we work for it. The "work" we must do is to remain present, open and willing to see the light again. The muddy little lotus doesn't worry if it will become a radiant flower once again. It knows this to be the Ultimate Truth. We do too, deep inside of us.

The daily practice of meditation, sitting quietly, connecting with my Higher Power, allows me to gain perspective of my human trials and triumphs. Thoughts come in and thoughts pass through my mind, like clouds in the sky. None of them mean anything more than the meaning I give them. By just showing up each day to connect, to be still and to open my heart, I allow God's love to come to me and through me. I allow the Light to call forth my muddy, little humanness into the magnificent, powerful Spirit that I am. I unclench my fist; the things I hold on to so tightly. I release and let go. I surrender to the One Divine Mind, knowing that the Light is always there for me to unfold into.

The Light, the Joy, the Peace is always there for you too. Be still. Show up every day to connect with the deepest part of who you truly are. Release your preconceived notions of how the world should be. Allow the great Sunshine of Spirit to call forth your muddy, little humanness, into the radiant beautiful being you already are.

Carol Hasbrouck is a consummate student of life and love. She's been a successful businesswoman in the financial arena, a motivational speaker, a published author, Chief Passion Officer of a small business focused on helping people Live Life on Purpose, and former CEO of Dames Gone Wild, a business dedicated to serving others. She is currently offering a brand new, highly effective Facebook marketing system called K.I.S.S. – Keep It Simple & Sustainable. Check it out at www.theclientqueen.com. Her most recent passion is Dance Walking. You may spot her around town, getting her groove on, with her happy go lucky dog, Jimmy.

The NOW:
How I Lost My Head and Found My Heart Space

By Elasa Tina Tiernan Sherbs

"The space in my heart holds the driver's key to my vehicle of the universe. And this key only ignites in the present moment."

I was born to a set of parents whose definition of God was unique. My mother could be found in nature or on the shore contemplating and meditating with the sun and all of nature, while my father, who walked as a human angel and literally was born in a plane midair, showed me that God hid in the most obscure places, such as a homeless man's words or a flower in the garden. Later in life, I came to the broad understanding that there are many paths leading to many understandings of creator, but I still wondered how I could live a life fully connected to creator, as creator, and through creator.

So I prayed to God to show me a way to get in touch with my own inner God spark, that simple SOUL choosing to show up authentically unique and undefined. It was the summer of 2004, and I had just assisted opening a string of spiritual centers. I knew I needed to shake off the daily scheduling created by life, bills, and career, and the cobwebs of mass-mind conditioning regarding what it means to be spiritual. I desired to feel more confidence in my shear Creative Being, the true form of god(dess) and creation.

I needed a sabbatical! So I closed up the center I was running with a note to clients that I would be heading west, with a light load, and with great love would return at the perfect time. On July 4th, what I like to call "INNER Dependence Day," I was off. I was guided by spirit to have NO PLAN, and to be in the NOW with a knowing that there would be "no wrong turns." My journey took me to spiritual communities, ashrams, parks, and hidden sages in oddest of places. As I reached the West Coast I could feel a freedom that was joyful and untethered. After several weeks I made my way to San Francisco and found a dear friend from college who needed guidance and offered a place to stay. While sharing my journeys with this friend and another, I told the ladies to sit down with me and do some finger painting to connect with their inner child. I asked to them to speak only in sounds, the language of love, while we painted. This led laughter and joy, as the sounds that could be heard were "ah, oh, ee, ie…" Something then moved within me to say, "Now Great Spirit please tell me what my soul's name is?!" The next three sounds I painted in song were E, La, Sa. My being became alive with light as the other two spoke their soul names ToSaLa, and LoLa.

When we finished, I immediately called my mother to tell her the news and, with great surprise, she loved it! We immediately began a search to find out more about Elasa: Goddess of Light and Truth, and we discovered that her story took place before time BEGAN (key point here). Elasa was being chased by a demon named Tien. He wanted her third eye as it held the keys to TRUTH. Tien chased Elasa down to the underworld, and finally captured her. He held her by the hair and drew his sword to cut her head off and have her third eye. Right before he made the cut she looked Tien in the eyes and laughed as she reminded him that she is eternal. As he took her head, out of her neck came eight beams of light that froze the demons in the land, transmuting the darkness. And then TIME BEGAN.

Just as I read this part of the story to my mother over the phone, a book from the top shelf at my friend's house fell to the floor. My mother and I laughed and quickly said aloud, "flip turn!!" I told her to hold on and I got the book, which was titled *The Mind's Eye*. I did a flip turn to chapter 2: "The Day I Lost My Head." In brief, the author described how she finally lost her head and got into her heart space while meditating on sabbatical in the Himalayas. At this moment, NOW TIME began for her, and she experienced deep peace and an understanding of the PRESENCE of God that can be felt in the present moment.

Since connecting with the soul name of Elasa, and finding that I AM the God Spark when in a state of free flowing creativity bound by nothing, I have become conscious that it is my participation in the present moment that defines co-creation. It is where the masculine practice of being consciously connected to the true *you* blends with the feminine brilliance of being open to the light and freedom of undefined creativity and synchronicity.

My offering to you dear fellow god(dess) spark is to greet

your day with a prayer and intention to be connected to that the god(dess) spark. Then move through your day open to the possibilities of the divine canvas called life as you unfold your soul's masterpieces and creations.

Try this practice: Choose a day that plans, schedules, and normal routines can be released. Pack a few super-food snacks such as nuts, fruits, vegetables, and water. Head to your favorite nature spot for a short 10-20 minute meditation and intention setting session. Set your intention to be connected to your god(dess) spark, and to be guided by this super conscious part of yourself to connect to the appropriate people and places to further assist in awakening you to your path, purpose, and truth.

For this day or time period, focus on being super present in the moment, and pay attention to the "characters" that connect with you, the messages that come forth from the nature kingdom, and events that unfold. Move forward in the direction of what feels right in your heart. Be open to the possibility that you may choose to stay put at the nature oasis of choice, or your journey may lead you to unfold mysteries from within the entirety of consciousness. And enjoy your time in The NOW!

Rev. Elasa Tina Marie Tiernan OT, CYT had a near death experience at the age of 10 that awakened her to the healing arts. She began reading books on Energy Medicine and knew that she would assist many on the realization of the SOUL. She studied western medicine at University of Florida and practices CranioSacral Therapy, Reiki, and Yoga. She also co-leads God(dess) Retreats. Her private Soul Star Source Practice is in Palm Harbor, FL. She is currently teaching Sol Energetic and Meditation Training, Essential Oil Yoga, Healing Facilitation Certifications, and Yoga via the web and around the globe. Visit www.SoulStarSource.com or www.sol-terra.guru.

The Awakening of Signs in a Synchronous Universe

By Camille Titone

The Universe provides you with every synchronicity you need to fully experience the world and receive the necessary instructions on how to best advance in your life. I believe there are no coincidences. Everything that is meant to occur in your lifetime will unfold in the proper "Spirit time."

When you notice the noticeable and are consciously "awake," additional synchronicities begin to occur. You possess an innate, intuitive knowledge within every cell of your present body and within your DNA from many previous lives. You are unique and have a mission(s) for this lifetime that is supremely special. In this 21st Century you are here for a higher purpose. It is the wise soul that takes notice of these synchronous occurrences in daily life. They come to us through nature, other people, and just about every important adventure in life when we are in a state of concentrated consciousness.

I have come to realize my life has been a series of special synchronicities. One sacred occurrence took place in 1981 at Rockaway Beach in Queens, NY. On a warm, bright and sunny Sunday, the feast day of St. Francis of Assisi, I found a worn, gray sand dollar shell, and it opened an unfolding of events that continued for several hours.

At the beach that day I played a little game, silently saying, "I will not pick up any shells today." "I will just walk, talk, and play with You in song and dance, my Lord." In the next moment, as if a bolt of lightning struck the sand, my eye caught sight of a shiny speck. In awe and wonder, I felt compelled to possess this small round shell. Now, fixed with a conundrum, as I had just promised a second ago not to pick up any shells, I slowly and attentively, in a 360-degree circle, surrounded the spot where the speck was covered by sand. Aware that God is All-loving, I picked up my newfound contentment. Time stood still, ever so briefly, as a connection to this sand dollar left me in an ethereal state of mind. I knew this day would be etched in my heart, mind, and soul forever.

After my walk at the shore, I took a short but deep sleep on the sand. Following a conversational dream I woke up stating, "Yes, I will write the book!" Afterward, I picked up my belongings, shoes, and shell and left the beach for the day. Getting in my car, deciding to keep the sand dollar close, I held it between my thumb and forefinger. As I backed out of the parking spot, to my disappointment, the shell broke into two perfectly jagged halves.

Three years later, another synchronicity! I found "The Legend of the Sand Dollar," which explains that the sand dollar is representative of Christ and many times is referred to as the Holy Ghost shell. The markings on a Sand Dollar represent the birth, death, and resurrection of Christ. The legend states: When the shell is broken open the Holy Spirit descends upon you. I realized this occurred the very day I found my shell. I was elated. However, after many attempts at writing, not knowing what to share, my life moved on.

The same year, I had a dream one night that I can still envision in my mind to this day. I woke with my hands crisscrossed at my breast and said aloud, "If I never believed before my Lord, I do now." In my dream, I was in a boat in the middle of a dark ocean, in a raging storm. A figure with a bright yellow slicker beckoned me to take the helm, which was spinning out of control as we stood on the deck. I still recall the recoiled and hesitant "No!" barely whispered. The figure stretched his hand out over the swelling sea. Looking down into the waves I saw white, ghostlike faces with horrific expressions. All were drowning as their outstretched arms were reaching up toward me. The dream was a powerful message, but I woke up and life moved on.

Although, it was not immediately apparent — in fact, the time span was exactly 10 years — I did come to believe it was my responsibility to help save humanity. These experiences and dreams took me on a journey that led me to strive for perfection on a daily basis. Then, suddenly, the synchronicities were rapidly increasing — so much so that I could no longer comprehend or trust the information I was receiving. I became truly confused and discontent. My life experience for nearly the next 20 years was an agonizing downward spiral. I fully realized during that extensive span of time that I could not find perfection as a human being on earth and become an enlightened being. It was not my destiny at this time. I also came to understand that I am on a journey and synchronicity is the roadmap for growth not a destination marker for enlightenment.

If I can leave you with one sincere idea, it would be to look to the synchronicities in your life, both large and small, and to take them seriously. Reflect on them daily and understand that they are signals and signs from the Universe. Be full of hope and direction, for within us all is the Christ Consciousness.

Camille Titone's motives are altruistic. She has a love for all humanity. As young as three years old her life was in the realm of Dance. She veered from a creative path beginning a career in the corporate world. Camille left her comfortable position to search a path more true to her life mission(s). Camille considers herself a "late bloomer." This is her first published work in this collaborative effort to get her story out and in the hands of transformational readers. Her website is www. LoveAlwaysInBloom.com Please stop by, Camille would enjoy hearing your comments to her chapter on synchronicities.

Awake, Alive and Ready to Thrive

By Alison J. Kay

"Wow Ms. Kay, that's totally cool! I wanna do that too!"

"Ok Jeremy, hold on, let me make sure everyone saw it first, and then everyone can watch again. Ok," I redirected my focus back to the group of middle school boys and girls standing outside next to the row of bushes and trees in the corner of the schoolyard, where I had taken them.

"So who didn't see that, or wants to see it again?"

"Me!"

"Me too!"

"I wasn't able to see it when you walked by the bushes, but I saw the tree move! Will you do that thing with the tree again?"

A few of the boys pushed up from behind the front row of students so they could see better.

"Yeah, I wanna see the tree one again. That was cool!"

"But didn't you see the bushes too? That was even better. It was like she was a fan. The leaves were perfectly still until she got close to them, then they kinda softly waved as she walked by, and then they stopped after she'd walked by. It was like magic! You gotta see it! Seriously," Carlos announced to the group.

The group was an after school club that my friend and fellow Language Arts teacher, Mr. R, had agreed to facilitate with me. In our "Stress Reduction Club" I taught them yoga, meditation, Chi Gong, and some basics about how to work with the subtle energies, while Mr. R assisted. I have formal training as an energy medicine practitioner, blending five different modalities, as a: meditation teacher, yoga instructor, Chi Gong teacher, personal trainer, and Holistic Life Coach, PhD. Our "Stress Reduction Club" took place before I moved to Asia for a decade to study subtle energies. At that time, the combination of energy medicine, yoga and meditation, and holistic life coaching was my part-time business outside of teaching. So, Mr. R. wanted to deepen his understanding of these practices by assisting in the club.

We did a bit of each of these practices with the students, most of whom were boys, surprisingly. I remember that some of this was due to Mr. R's and my reputation as the "cool" teachers, and his efforts to recruit some of our more active boys, the ones who had difficulty settling down to read and write.

So, I led the kids through meditation each time the club met (twice a week), and they were able to settle down rather easily. This was no surprise to me: After 21 years of teaching meditation to more kids than adults, I have found that kids—especially teens—really take to meditation. They seem to like to "go in" and have time with their minds. I wonder, too, if they intuitively sense the health benefits cultivated by the practice, before I even point out what is known by Buddhism and considered by the Dalai Lama and leading teachers and practitioners like myself, and now many Western scientists, as a "Science of the Mind." They seem to get it.

And the more intellectual and older high school students actually react the same way, although they seem to be able to wrap their brains around the science of it with some sense of… you know what?... As I write this, now having taught Western adults meditation for six years and kids for 15 years, I know that kids—no matter what age or level of intellect—really don't require scientific explanations or validation to accept meditation. They just take right to it naturally once they go through the standard learning curve, which applies to kids and adults alike.

Back to that day 15 years ago in the schoolyard. I was showing "The Stress Reduction" club members the Chi in all animate life, after we'd just meditated and done a bit of Chi Gong and yoga. I wanted them to see more tangibly the Chi, Prana, or Universal Life Force Energy that they were learning to access more of, once they'd experienced clearing out the mental chatter, and getting a sense of flowing energy within them through the yoga and Chi Gong. I also taught them a bit about how their limiting beliefs closed down and restricted the flow of certain energy centers in the human body, which are called chakras (which means "wheels" in Sanskrit). By tying these practices together in this unique way, I was now showing them how they could go beyond their own mind/self/"fields" and access the greater field of universal Chi.

When I was first asked in media interviews about this ability to sense the interconnectedness and interact with the subtle energies, I explained that, yes, it had been cultivated by me, and that I later lived in Asia for 10 years, moving there with the precise intention of learning how to work with subtle energies better so that I could improve my energy medicine practice with clients and the quality of my life overall. Yet, in reflection during one of these earlier media interviews, it helped me to see that this is naturally who I am. It seems like I've always done this since a little girl, going out daily and playing in the woods with my older brother, and then picking up meditation practice at 22.

The science of consciousness, and specifically morphic fields, as they're now referred to in science, I explore in my book *What if There's Nothing Wrong?*, written in my last of 10 years in Asia. Yet underlying and beyond the scientific explanation is the experiential understanding that this first group of teens experienced. I turned them onto this idea of us existing in a world that is alive, and all is interconnected, and they weren't the same after. When reading this it's just words; when experiencing it, you can't remain the same because of this knowing that results from experiencing these sensations. If the mind requires explanation, it's now there; but the belief and trust and life choices come from the experience.

This awareness seems to bring so much relief to both kids and adults. If we can, in fact, Observe ourselves thinking when in meditation, and then redirect our focus back to our breath, then we can ask, "Who is doing this Observing and disciplining of the mind?" And once we recognize that we are not just this self-contained, self-absorbed thought factory, we can then move beyond the everyday mind and connect with the brilliant, beautiful, supportive energies that are all around us, at all times.

In my view, it is just a choice to stay shut down, only half alive, and barely awake. There is so much more aliveness, awakeness and energy abounding that if we spend one minute in depression—a.k.a. to me as "Self-suppression"—then it's one minute too many! Ooh, there it is, a thought about tomorrow; it's just simply "thinking," as the mind does. Come off of the thought and back to the breath, to the here and now. And in this redirection you will cultivate presence and be present. All the better to be able to create your best lives ever!

When we're connected to Source energy and when we work with consciousness instead of staying closed down to it and stuck in our minds— "figuring stuff out" and "making stuff happen" everything is not so difficult. Why choose that, when you can have ease and celebration? Duh.

Alison J. Kay, PhD is a Holistic Life Coach, an India trained YA Yoga & Meditation teacher, an ACE Certified Personal Trainer, and an energy medicine healer/shifter of 18 years nicknamed "the lightning bolt" due to the power of her energy. The unique blend of credentials, use of multiple modalities, and the experience she acquired during the 10 years she spent in Asia studying subtle energy practices, make her incredibly powerful. She is a former Talk Radio host of, "Create Your Best Life Ever! What Else is Possible?" which was in the top ten on the mind-body-spirit 7th Wave Channel of voiceamerica. com. Dr. Kay is the author of *What If There's Nothing Wrong?* Visit www.AlisonJKay.com.

The 3 Key Elements for Empowered Thriving

By Janice Carlin

None of us want to just live in this world. We want to thrive! And we want to see our children thriving as well. Unfortunately, a great majority of us are not experiencing this. Instead we find ourselves sick, anxious, depressed, struggling, and hopeless. I know what it is like to live this way, and I also know what it is like to shift to a different life — one filled with peace, joy, and vitality.

As a result of my own personal journey of healing and awakening, I have discovered three key elements to thriving. When you know about them, you become empowered to shift your experiences quickly and easily away from the struggles to what you desire.

Key #1: Know Who You Really Are

Who you are is not your body or your mind. Who you are is your soul. You *are* your soul, and you *have* a body and mind through which you experience thoughts and feelings and have experiences on Earth. This being said, you, as an individual being, have a certain soul energy. Additionally, you carry within yourself unique experiences, knowledge, and mastery. No matter where you live, what you look like, or the situations you find yourself experiencing in your life, your soul remains who/what your soul is and always has been — a unique facet of the entirety of all.

The reason that knowing all of this is so important is that it will allow you to step completely out of the limiting mindset of diagnostic labels and societal expectations. Here is an example of how this works: If you are an angelic being who has incarnated with a human body for the first time, the needs you will have for thriving will be different than one who has much experience incarnating as a human being. You will be more sensitive to the toxins, pathogens, and violence that exist here on Earth because you have never been exposed to them before. Therefore, when you start to react to them, rather than judging yourself or allowing someone else to judge you as sickly, weak, over-emotional, or mentally unstable, you can remember that the reason you are feeling badly is because you are a pure being of light who has been exposed to something toxic. And what can you do about it? That is what the next two keys are all about!

Key #2: Know How Energy Works In Our World

From the 5 percent of energy we see to the 95 percent we cannot see with our eyes—we are interacting with energy, and we are part of it. About 80 percent comprises dark matter (so-called because it cannot be seen), which actually moves around us and through us all the time.

Unfortunately, we have been gravely misled about how the energy we cannot see affects us. For example, consider an apple, which any doctor or nutritionist would say is part of a healthy diet. Here is what they do not say: If that apple has been conventionally grown, you also will be ingesting the following along with it—over 40 different types of pesticides, antibiotics, and chemical herbicides. In addition to the energy in our polluted food, water, and air, we are exposed to EMFs (electromagnetic fields) from electronics and the emotional energy of violent thoughts and acts all around us. What we cannot see most definitely can hurt us.

Toxic energies abound on Earth because people create, produce, and use them. You have to be diligent upon keeping them away from you if you want to feel good and live to your highest potential. This includes what you ingest, inhale, and place upon your body. It also includes the rest of the unseen energies in any space where you are, and within and around your body. You can work to eliminate the toxic energies from your life that are within your control by eating organic food, refraining from smoking, and using natural household cleaners and body products. In order to keep the rest from hurting you, you have to know about the third key.

Key #3 Know How to Work Effectively With Energy

People can learn to work with energy to help themselves thrive. Your soul works harmoniously with your body to convey information to you. Therefore, if you feel badly (emotionally, physically, or having negative thoughts), then you have come into contact with a toxic energy. Some people are naturally able to detoxify these energies without much effort, while others have to do more exercise or drink green juices to move the energies out and away from themselves. Some have to add subtle energy clearing techniques along with physical detox protocols to remain in a healthy state. I fall into this category, as does my highly sensitive son. This is because of who we are on a soul level. Energy clearing techniques are simple, accessible, and free to use. Even kids can do them easily. Doreen Virtue, Ph.D., shares many powerful, gentle techniques in her books, as do I.

When you work intentionally with energy, you can more easily manifest what you desire. You will find that you can step into the driver's seat and move from passively living to actively creating and thriving. When you learn to work with energy on multiple levels simultaneously, you honor yourself because this is how you truly exist. It is easy to slap a label on people who are not able to thrive to their highest potential. But doing this does not solve the issues causing the problems in the first place. If you or your child is struggling, consider if you are addressing all three key elements as deeply as possible. Look for helpful, quality resources that you trust, and enjoy stepping into your power to heal, shift, and transform your life yourself.

Janice Carlin is an intuitive channel and the author of *The Sensitivity Factor, Be Free, Toward Ascension, Empathic Sensitivity,* and *The Foundations Healing System Guidebook,* a revolutionary healing system she developed for highly sensitive people. She is passionate about sharing information that empowers people to care for themselves, their children and the Earth in the most honoring ways possible. She has a Master's degree in music and is a certified Holographic Sound Healing practitioner. A leader in teaching the direct links between science and spirituality, which empower people in their everyday lives, she can be found at Empowered Thriving, www.janicecarlin.com.

The Insurance Policy

By Scott Allen

I could have died yesterday...Great way to start a story, right? Very dramatic, but also true. If you think about it, any one of us could have died yesterday, whether from a massive stroke, a car wreck or, as in my case, a simple trip-and-fall incident. "Stuff" happens, and that is when you are glad you have an insurance policy. I'll get back to that later...

Not long ago I'm helping my better half move some furniture. She has a home staging business, so it is not uncommon for me, or her family and friends, to help move home decor from time to time. We all know the risk in helping is usually just the possibility of sore muscles the next day, certainly not the risk of death or serious injury.

So here's the story: I was carrying a heavy, awkwardly shaped table out the front door to the borrowed-for-the-day pickup truck. For some unknown reason, the builder of the house included a booby-trap 3-inch-high step to the landing at the front door. Pavers of the same color as the sidewalk camouflage this step. Immediately to the left of the sidewalk is a 2-foot-high concrete block decorative retaining wall for the planter in front of the house.

You probably already know where this is headed. Sure enough, I did not see the step as I was leaving the house carrying the table on my right side, and I stepped onto 3 inches of "air." Okay, I know that doesn't sound like a big deal, but carrying the heavy table, and not being a kid anymore, I could have been stepping off the edge of the Grand Canyon the way my body was flung to the left into—you guessed it—the 2-foot-high concrete wall.

The left side of my rib cage became the perfect target area for the sharp edge of the blocks. Anyone who has ever watched a football game has seen the "hit to the ribs" delivered by a defensive back to the wide receiver stretched out reaching to catch a ball. Now I haven't played football since Pop Warner, and I never was a wide receiver, but I now know how those guys must feel.

I lay there stunned and literally could not breathe for what seemed like several minutes. I am sure it was probably really only a minute or so, but I am not kidding when I say I could not breathe. Funny thing when you cannot breathe, you really, really want to!

Of course my better half comes over and says those oh-so-helpful words in that moment: "Can you breathe?!?" OK, I know, I know, I probably would have said the same thing, or maybe the other classic, "Are you hurt?" For the record, my answers in this case were "No" and "Yes." As I was lying there for those 60 seconds, it did cross my mind that I might really be hurt, and what if I can't breathe for something like five or 10 minutes. That would be, as they say in the medical field, *Not Good*.

Since you are reading this story, you already got the spoiler alert that I was, in fact, able to start breathing again. That was, in medical terms, a *Good Thing*. After a few minutes I could be helped up and, since I was not bleeding and no bones were protruding, just like in football, I walked it off. Five minutes after that, we were back to loading furniture.

We had two vehicles, and as I was driving the truck back to our storage unit, my mind started to wander as my ribs really started to ache. What if that wall was just a little farther out and, instead of my ribs, I took that blow to the side of my head. There is no doubt in my mind if that were the case, I would not be writing this story, and I might not have written anything again—ever. I could have "checked out" then and there, not doing anything stupid or reckless; It would have been "like being hit by a bus"—here one moment and gone the next.

It got me musing about the concept of mortality and our "purpose" in life. In the book *10 Secrets for Success and Inner Peace*, author Wayne Dyer states that when we die we cannot not take any of our possessions with us. What we leave behind is our life's work. He says, "You'll find yourself feeling purposeful if you can find a way to always be in the service of others."

Pablo Picasso was quoted as saying,

"The meaning of life is to find your gift. The purpose of life is to give it away."

Many people know the famous quote from Winston Churchill, "We make a living by what we get, but we make a life by what we give."

I certainly agree with Wayne, Pablo, and Winston. And I want to add what I call "The Round World Concept," which I define as doing good things for others and it will come back to you multiplied. We all want to be remembered for the good deeds we did, the "random acts of kindness," and being there for another person.

Many like-minded people are taking action by joining a service club, volunteering, or just lending a helping hand to another person. In a way, these service acts are like premiums paid into the Universe's insurance policy. When we are down, there will be someone or something there to pick us up. Perhaps the policy even goes so far as a Higher Power metaphorically assuring that a "wall" you hit one day may certainly get your attention, but will leave nothing more serious than a bruise to the ribs.

Perhaps everyone should start conducting a Universe insurance policy check-up. In the process, don't just **think** about acts of service. Get active and **do** something for a friend or, better yet, a stranger or, even better, your community. Consider one more quote from John Burroughs: "The smallest deed is better than the greatest intention."

Be the person who does good deeds for others. Humanity will be better because of your efforts, and the Universe may just find a way to insure that when you need it, you're covered as well.

Scott Allen has a Bachelor's Degree from Florida Southern College, with training in the social sciences. Scott is an entrepreneur, writer, artist and father of three magnificent sons. He is also a practitioner of New Thought and his dedication to "ARKs" (Acts of Random Kindness) was documented in a television news segment. He is a charter member of The Burg Exchange Club and was Co-Chairperson of the Toss Out Hunger Fundraising Committee benefiting local children in need. A contributing author and columnist to multiple publications, he can be reached at jcotinc@gmail.com.

Clearing the Path to Abundance

By Rev. Spencer Rouse

Most of us have hang-ups in some areas of our lives, and career, money and love are at the top of the list based on my work over many years. It's hard to face these issues, so we typically rationalize or ignore our shortcomings. We have formed energy blockages to protect us from experiencing emotional pain, much of it from childhood. As we mature, these blockages are responsible for false and mixed messages that keep us stuck, confused, and unable or unwilling to manifest and maintain happiness, fulfillment and abundance in life. However, with the right understanding we can change these patterns, and there are some simple steps that will help lead us down the right path.

Blocks to Career and Financial Success

If we are not achieving on a career path, the reasons are often rooted in our perceptions, not in fact. Religious teachings or family culture might have instilled "mental programs" in us that are not valid, but they control us anyway. "Pride goeth before a fall." This phrase can guilt us into being embarrassed by our successes, for instance. Instead of allowing enthusiasm to propel us, we hold back, not wanting to stand out.

Women, especially, can hold onto fear of success surrounding business and career advancement. There are a variety of hidden messages that can sabotage their efforts to move forward. Family training may have instilled beliefs that business success is for men only, even while the same families are setting high performance standards in education.

We also may fear that if we are very successful, we are cheating others from their share of "the pie." A "mental program" runs through many repeating that there is not enough "out there" for everyone. Only the pushy few can rise to the top. This implies sacrifices and the inability to have a healthy, balanced lifestyle. It also can activate conflicting hidden beliefs about the importance of money, and a personal unworthiness "program" instilled by certain types of religious training.

Moreover, sometimes we are stalemated financially from fear of lack. Many of us have immigrant ancestors who had to struggle to survive. Our parents or grandparents had concerns about having enough money for food, shelter and clothing during the Great Depression. Some of these fears were altered and passed down to the next generations as misguided approaches regarding money and its flow in our lives. We have been trained as a nation to respect, crave, or idolize money, but this often comes with hidden fears and conflicting messages.

Breaking Barriers to Find Love

When we look for love, we are often looking for respect, acceptance, admiration, confirmation of worthiness, and validation of ourselves, as well as companionship, material security, etc. When we hold onto resentments, a victim mentality, or confusion about our own feelings regarding ourselves, these traits are reflected in our personalities. We develop irrational fears based on mixed and confusing messages from deep inside. We try to avoid hurt. We are afraid. We cannot access our feelings and, as a result, we block ourselves from understanding what will help us find fulfillment in love.

Fear of failure or rejection can keep us from pursuing goals of any kind. Holding onto anger and resentment from the past puts up blocks. When we are so concerned that we might fail, we do not give ourselves space for success. We look at the negative and hesitate to take the chances that will bring new experiences into our lives. We get stuck. Once we understand that feeling worthy is a mindset, and there is abundance enough for everyone, we are ready to look at what has blocked our success in the past and remove it.

The Road to Removing Blockages

There are a variety of techniques that can help us come to terms with almost any blockage, regardless of the root cause. First, sit in meditation and breathe deeply. Ask for inspiration to help with your problem, but do not try to control it. The answer may come to you the next day or the next week. It will be subtle, so pay attention. Keep up this practice and you will be amazed at the insights gained.

You also have the ability to create abundance if you understand the principles of manifesting. In brief: Know what you want. Keep the vibration of what you want very pure. Do not dilute it with an undercurrent of doubt, anxiety, disbelief or anything else negative. Draw the desired situation to you using the energy *from the heart and not the mind*. Make sure you are in energetic alignment with what you want. Expect success and have motivation that is founded in *helping all rather than seeking selfish gain*.

If you cannot push through a blockage easily, working with muscle testing or practices such as meridian tapping (Emotional Freedom Technique) can help move specific issues into the foreground so you can view them and yourself from a new perspective. Once you can consciously face an issue, it most likely will begin to dissolve.

Affirmations are another way to break up "mental programs." You can use a general one, "I am healthy, wealthy, and wise" or "If anyone can do it, I can do it." These replace negative mind chatter with positive thoughts. You may add details to attract something specific, "I have $500 to pay my bill by the due date." As long as the affirmations are aligned with what you really want at a soul level (from the heart), repeating them can bring positive things into your life. However, do not try to draw a specific person into your life; this interferes with power of choice. State desired qualities instead. Hypnosis, therapy, and intuitive readings also can shed light on issues that are difficult to uncover. Experiment with a combination of techniques until you dissolve your blockages and begin to feel the freedom that is your birthright.

While we all have our weak points, we each have the potential to draw to us what we need to live a rich, full life and to make peace with ourselves. The key is to take charge of our own life and take action now!

Rev. Spencer Rouse has been a psychic medium, teacher, counselor, writer, musician, and healer for more than 25 years. She completed Level 1 and 2 studies in Acoustic Sound, Color, and Body Movement with Fabien Maman (Father of Vibrational Sound Therapy) at the Tama-do Academy in Malibu, CA, and Switzerland. Spencer writes, lectures, and teaches self-discovery by tuning into the true self through the tools of sound, color, and ancient teachings. For more information visit www.PsychicSpencer.com or email PsychicSpencer@yahoo.com.

The Precious Present: Learning to Live in the Moment

By Howard Peiper

Life unfolds in the present. But so often, we let the present slip away, by allowing time to rush past unobserved and unseized, and by squandering the precious seconds of our lives as we worry about the future and ruminate about what's past. When we are at work, we fantasize about being on vacation and, when we finally take that trip, we worry about the work piling up on our desks. We dwell on intrusive memories of the past or fret about what may or may not happen in the future.

We need to live more in the moment. Living in the moment (also called mindfulness) is a state of active, open, intentional attention on the present. When we become mindful, we realize that we are not our thoughts; we become an observer of our thoughts from moment to moment without judging them. Mindfulness involves being with our thoughts as they are, neither grasping at them nor pushing them away. Instead of letting our life go by without living it, we awaken to experience.

Cultivating a nonjudgmental awareness of the present bestows a host of benefits. Mindfulness reduces stress, boosts immune functioning, reduces chronic pain, lowers blood pressure, and helps patients cope with cancer. By alleviating stress, spending a few minutes a day actively focusing on living in the moment even reduces the risk of heart disease.

Follow the Path

There are many paths to mindfulness — and at the core of each is a paradox. Ironically, letting go of what we want is the only way to get it. Here are some other suggestions:

1. **To improve our performance, stop thinking about it (unself-consciousness).** That's the first paradox of living in the moment. Thinking too hard about what we're doing actually makes us do

worse. If we are in a situation that makes us anxious—giving a speech, introducing ourselves to a stranger, dancing—focusing on our anxiety tends to heighten it. Focus less on what is going on in our mind and more on what is going on in the room, less on our mental chatter and more on ourselves as part of something.

2. **To avoid worrying about the future, focus on the present (savoring).** Often we're so trapped in thoughts of the future or the past that we forget to experience, let alone enjoy, what is happening right now. When subjects in a study took a few minutes each day to actively savor something they usually hurried through (eating a meal, drinking a cup of tea, walking to the bus) they began experiencing more joy, happiness and positive emotions, and fewer depressive symptoms. The hallmark of depression and anxiety is "catastrophizing," which means worrying about something that hasn't happened yet and might not happen at all. Worry, by its very nature, means thinking about the future, and if we hoist ourselves into awareness of the present moment, worrying melts away.

3. **To make the most of time, lose track of it (flow).** Perhaps the most complete way of living in the moment is the state of total absorption or flow. Flow occurs when we are so engrossed in a task that we lose track of everything else around us. Flow is an elusive state. As with romance or sleep, we can't just will ourselves into it, all we can do is set the stage, creating the optimal conditions for it to occur.

4. **If something is bothering us, move toward it, rather than away from it (acceptance).** We all have pain in our lives, whether it's the ex we still long for, the jackhammer snarling across the street, or the sudden waves of anxiety when we get up to give a speech. If we let them, such irritants can distract us from the enjoyment of life. The mind's natural tendency when faced with pain is to attempt to avoid it by trying to resist unpleasant thoughts, feelings and sensations. Acceptance of an unpleasant state doesn't mean we don't have goals for the future. It just means we accept that certain things are beyond our control. The sadness, stress, pain or anger is there whether we like it or not. Better to embrace the feeling as it is. Nor does acceptance mean we have to like what is happening.

Living a consistently mindful life takes effort. But mindfulness itself is easy. Mindfulness is the only intentional, systematic activity that is not about trying to improve ourselves or get anywhere else. It is simply a matter of realizing where we already are. We can become mindful at any moment just by paying attention to our immediate experience. We can do it right now. What is happening this instant? Think of the "self" as an eternal witness, and just observe the moment. What do we see, hear or smell? It doesn't matter how it feels (pleasant or unpleasant, good or bad). We roll with it because it's what is present; we are not judging it. And if we notice our mind wandering, bring ourselves back. Just say to our self, "Now, Now, Now."

Remember, when we are living in the moment that is our precious present.

Precious Present

By Meg Cassell

*A moment of quiet in the midst of life
Envelopes me in a soft flow
Of Being.*

*It juxtaposes itself suddenly.
The world
Stops.*

*Gliding in, it is sweet and sublime,
Catching me off-guard.
Fleeting.*

*My thoughts then resume
Their characteristic chaos,
Their normal pace.
Where have I just been?
Accidental mindfulness, gift or chance,
It was enchanted space,
Filled not with detached indifference*

*But with
Intense
Peace.
An awe-filled moment of Totality,
Immersion
In Love
As big as the universe.*

*A moment of quiet in the midst of life
Envelopes me in a soft flow.
It is a
Precious
Present.*

Meg Cassell is an accomplished professional classical musician who loves to write poetry. She regularly uses Twitter as a poetry microblog and can be found @ TweetKuPoetry. Her themes are generally about life, love, and the return to our innate wholeness and divinity.

Dr. Howard Peiper is a nationally recognized expert in the holistic counseling field. His healing, health care and natural professional credentials extend over a thirty year period and include those of naturopath, author, lecturer, magazine consultant, radio personality and host of a television show. Howard, nominated for a Pulitzer Prize, has written numerous books on nutrition and natural health including 12 best sellers. Dr. Peiper is co-host of the award winning television show, *Partners in Healing*. They feature guests in the alternative healing field including such names as Harvey Diamond, Dr. John Upledger, Dr. Bernard Jensen, Gary Null and Dr. Marshall Mandell. Visit drhowardpeiper.wordpress.com.

A Drop Named Splendid: Remembering Oneness

By Emily Rivera

"All know that the drop merges into the ocean, but few know that the ocean merges into the drop." – Kabir

Once upon a time there was a drop named Splendid. This little drop knew itself to be the ocean. It knew not of itself in any other way. Splendid moved with ease through the sea and through the many elements that embodied the ocean. She witnessed the different components, but consciously couldn't distinguish any separation from the all. She was ocean and wonder, creatures and rocks, sand and breeze.

One day Splendid felt a stir through the Ocean with great power…The Sun had spoken; with its voice came rays of light which casted themselves upon the Sea. A particular ray moved graciously towards Splendid with ripples of warmth that surrounded her essence, and she felt loved. Sun spoke directly to Splendid with gentle love and power. It told her about the Ocean, and of the earth that connected with the sea. It shared that the Ocean and earth were one of the same, just unique components of the whole. Splendid, fueled with wonder, asked question after question of this place, and for the first time she felt the energy of desire move through the ripples of her being. She wished to experience herself though the elements of earth. In loving response to this sincere desire, the Sun stretched its rays beyond the sea and in one swift move brought them all together to create a perfect circle of light.

Sun apprised Splendid that she was to become a drop of water and that she would journey through earth within this circle of light; and with this truth she'd always be protected and guided by the light. In the Sun's love she became enlightened within the awareness that she is part of the Ocean and Sea, water and light in its unison, earth and sky just the same, and free to be all that she pleased. Sun then spoke once again, and all time seized as Splendid the drop got carried up, up, up into the sky; and with a gentle breeze brought forth through the breathe of all creation, she became one with the clouds.

Splendid was filled with awe as she witnessed the beauty and perfection contained within the deep emerald blue Ocean, and for the first time she knew herself as free.

The bliss exalted her higher into the sky, heightening her understanding of it all. With the light as her guide and the Sun's essence as her companion, she was in perfect alignment; and within that instant...Swish...She felt herself fall.

Falling faster and faster though the sky, past the clouds that welcomed her in this ordained initiation, past the blue that she once knew herself to be. Falling steadfastly through the uninhibited air that filled the space between sky and earth, her ultimate destination; Earth, a place that Sun had inspired for her to see. Splendid, full of eagerness to what may unfold. At last finding herself moving amongst colors she had never seen and finalizing her fall into the arms of a wide opened Lillie that, unbeknownst to its awareness, was expecting Splendid's sudden arrival.

Lillie moved with the wind, yet unaware of Splendid's presence and her light. Splendid felt herself gently gliding down Lillie's petal propelled by a hidden force that she didn't recognize but one that contained the same warmth and love she felt from the Sun. Lillie depends on drops like Splendid to maintain her physical existence, and in that visit Splendid would be offering life to Lillie while empowering her growth. Shivers of sustenance moved through Lillie as she discovered Splendid's presence and the good she was bringing forth. Splendid, without effort, felt an aspect of her break away. A new drop emerged and it moved further down Lillie's petals and ultimately down into the ground. Lillie felt joy and in her presence and expressed gratitude for the gift Splendid had just bestowed.

Splendid felt elated, for in this moment she knew herself as Love, and in this she felt bliss. Moments passed and the breeze brought Splendid to the tip of Lillie's perimeters and, with a blink of an eye, Splendid found herself being carried up in the sky by a creature with intricate wings and vivid colors. Butterfly was this creature's name. He was bold and full of confidence. He recognized Splendid as a source of sustenance and depended on her now. She felt herself in disarray, since she felt no freedom in this moment. So she called on the light that was part of her whole and she noticed more drops falling from the sky upon her. They brought with them strength and inspiration and she felt herself grow. She received what was needed and what she had set forth through intention, and within that she found peace. Butterfly landed on the side of a tree, in which he proceeded to drink from Splendid's new expanded self.

In this moment, Splendid knew herself as nourishment, and in this she felt bliss.

Butterfly now carried her further in his arms over a river that was part of this land. He let her go as he shared gratitude through his energy. In doing so, she could further be part of the Earth she was destined to see. Her excitement and experience of adventure elevated to its highest as she headed down the rapid river. This presence was joy, and within it she heard laughter. River was neither male nor female but one and the same and it played with Splendid with every bump and turn. River informed Splendid that it was happy to have her as a guest. It showed her different components of earth and the ultimate potentials contained through its banks. Splended felt herself grow in understanding. In turn, she shared with River all that she has learned and the experience with the Sun. River felt fortified in this knowledge.

In this moment, Splendid knew herself as Wisdom, and in this she felt bliss.

In a quick turn of the land, Splendid found herself being catapulted up into the sky. She saw Sun in its splendor and felt instantaneous bliss. In this moment she knew herself as Sun, as she graciously evaporated into its light and its rays. She had fully become part of the whole, neither Ocean nor drop, but one with it all. Sun chanted words of knowledge and love as it brought Splendid back to Ocean, as she once knew herself to be.

In this moment Splendid knew herself as complete, and in this she felt bliss.

Awaken to the Splendid within you. Know yourself as love, and in this truth you too will find your bliss.

Emily Rivera is a national speaker, consultant, and spiritual counselor who lectures on the power of eternal consciousness, energy, and serves as a channel for the Ascended Lights. Her popular events and readings offer insights and guidance to people all over the world. Her unique, multidimensional approach is truly empowering and brings forth exceptional clarity, healing, and inspiration for enhanced personal awareness and achievement. Emily knows we can change both our personal destiny, and that of human existence, when we awaken to our soul's potential. By applying her techniques for making direct connections with innate wisdom, many report being propelled into a powerful paradigm shift. Visit www.theangelcoach.com

Do YOU have a story to tell?

TRANSFORM YOUR LIFE!
Stories and Insights from Experts and Real Life Heroes

Get your copy of BOOK 2!

Find out how you can become a co-author in the *Transform Your Life!* Book Series!

Transform Your Life! is all about inspiring, empowering, providing practical tools, and sharing powerful stories of transformation, hope, and success. We want YOU to share your experience, journey, and wisdom and help guide readers to see life with limitless possibilities. Whether it's finding your purpose, learning about the power of the mind, overcoming life's obstacles, finding healing, staying inspired, loving yourself, or any number of other transformational topics, the content in *Transform Your Life!* leaves readers ready to make life long changes and improve their lives. By sharing your experience with others, you have the opportunity to change lives. *Transform Your Life!* is a mirror for people to see themselves—deep into their own soul—and learn from YOUR powerful lessons.

TRANSF✦RMATION
PUBLISHING

APPLY ONLINE AT: www.Transformation-Publishing.com/transformbook

Practical tools for transformation!